Therapy Without A Therapist

A DIY Guide to Good Mental Health & Growth
An updated new edition
(With a new introduction, and a revised and expanded
section on emotions)

Avigail Abarbanel

Fully Human Psychotherapy
http://fullyhuman.co.uk
'Fully Human Psychotherapy Tools for Life Series'
2017-2023

Therapy Without a Therapist
A DIY Guide to Good Mental Health & Growth

An Updated New Edition
(With a new introduction, and a revised and expanded
section on emotions)

'Fully Human Psychotherapy Tools for Life Series'

Other publications in the series:

Grief and Adjustment to Change: A no-nonsense approach

Do not Put Up With Anxiety: Cure it!

Trauma & Its Impact: What you need to know

Relationships: Why are they difficult & what can we do about it?

First published December 2020
(Updated: 06/09/2023)

This book is not intended as a substitute
for medical or psychological treatment.
It should not be used for diagnosis or treatment of any illness.
Please seek the advice and care of a professional
if you experience symptoms that worry you.

Acknowledgements

I am deeply grateful to Dr Daniel Siegel for his ongoing meticulous work, which has resulted in the development of the new framework of Interpersonal Neurobiology (IPNB). Dan's work has been a gamechanger for my profession. For the first time in the history of the profession, we can understand what the role of psychotherapy really is, explain it to our clients, and work more efficiently and robustly in partnership with them. I am infinitely grateful to my wise clinical supervisor, mentor and role model Annette Fisher who has always supported my development as a professional and as a person, and who has helped me think about my work from so many perspectives. I will forever be grateful to my great teachers, the late Dr David Jansen, and his wife and partner Margaret Newman for the incredible study opportunity they have offered me and my fellow students at the Jansen Newman Institute in Sydney in the late 1990s. What they taught me has provided a solid theoretical, practical, and ethical foundation that has guided my work since I qualified. I am grateful to all the clients I have met over the years, who have trusted me with their psychological development, and who have allowed me to accompany them on their journeys, and to witness their transformations. Your honest, ongoing feedback and insights on the work we have been doing together has been invaluable. Without you this book would not be possible. My deepest thanks to Dr Peter Carden for his help to create the graph on page 86. My gratitude to my insightful friend Johanna Schuster, a woman of many talents and gifts, who has proofread and offered useful comments on the first version of this manuscript. Last, but not least, my deepest thanks to Brendan Stephens, my supportive and loving partner, for helping with the editing of the manuscript, and for his suggestions and advice.

"All the evidence that we have ... indicates that ... in practically every human being and certainly in almost every newborn baby, that there is an active will toward health, and impulse toward growth, or toward the actualization of human potentialities. But at once we are confronted with the very saddening realization that so few people make it. Only a small proportion of the human population gets to the point of identity, of selfhood, full humanness, self-actualization, etc., even in a society like ours which is relatively one of the most fortunate on the face of the earth. This our great paradox. We have the impulse towards full development of humanness. Then why is it that it doesn't happen more often? What blocks it?" — A. Maslow (1971) *The Farther Reaches of Human Nature.* (pp. 24-25)

೪⊷ೀ

"The human being seems to require meaning. To live without meaning, goals, values, or ideals seems to provoke ... considerable distress. In severe form it may lead to the decision to end one's life." — I. D. Yalom (1980). *Existential Psychotherapy.* (p.422)

೪⊷ೀ

"When a system becomes integrated, it is the most flexible, adaptive, coherent, energized, and stable. ... This flow of energy and information that links separate elements together has the subjective experience of harmony. Like a choir singing "Amazing Grace", each singer retains his or her own individual voice while simultaneously linking together with intervals that drive the flow of the whole song. The sensation of harmony is the subjective side of the physical state of integration." — D. Siegel (2010). *The Mindful Therapist.* (p.31

Table of Contents

Introduction

Captain Jean-Luc Picard (to Ralph Offenhouse):

"A lot has changed in the past three hundred years. People are no longer obsessed with the accumulation of things. We've eliminated hunger, want, the need for possessions. We've grown out of our infancy." …

Ralph Offenhouse: "Then what is the challenge?"

Captain Jean-Luc Picard: "The challenge, Mr. Offenhouse, is to improve yourself. To enrich yourself. Enjoy it."

— *Star Trek, *The Next Generation*. (Episode: 'The Neutral Zone'. 1988).

People laugh when they read on my website that my goal as a psychotherapist is to make myself redundant. I do not blame them. Who in their right mind would want to do themselves out of a job in a society where almost everyone must make a living just to survive, and keep a roof over their heads? As you read on, I hope my reasons for aiming to make myself redundant will become obvious. In fact, this book is all about making psychotherapy obsolete.

When a car breaks and cannot fulfil its purpose, we take it to the mechanic to be fixed. If it is no longer fixable, we replace it with one that does, or find another solution for our transport needs. The same applies to any tool or gadget we use[1].

---

* For non-Star Trek fans: In this 1988 episode of *The Next Generation*, the star ship 'Enterprise' comes across cryogenic pods from the late Twentieth Century floating in space in a defunct vessel. When the three humans in them are thawed and healed, they find the 24th Century very different from the reality they remember. The conversation above is between the Captain, and Ralph Offenhouse, a late 20th Century fifty-five-year-old financier, whose whole life was about the accumulation of money and possessions.

[1] I am well aware of how problematic our 'throw away' culture is and how devastating it is to our environment and the planet. I use this example just to make a point, not to advocate that we throw things away!

What about humans? What are humans supposed to 'do', or 'be'? What are we, humans, *for*? The humanistic and existential therapeutic traditions on which I was trained do not view suffering human beings as 'broken objects' that need fixing, nor do they view therapists as 'technicians'. But the reality is that most, if not all, who come to therapy think there is something wrong with them, and that they need fixing. They believe their anxiety, depression, stress, or whatever else they suffer from is a sign that they are 'malfunctioning' psychologically.

I do not blame anyone for thinking this way. Somewhere deep-down people recognise they are more than the sum of their problems, and that there are valid reasons behind their suffering. But almost everyone around them, especially experts, encourage them to think of their psychological difficulties as a 'malfunction', an illness, a pathology.

Our society is utilitarian. It measures people by what they *do*, how well they can cope, not by who they are. Our feelings, hopes, aspirations, ideals, our need for love, and connection, for kindness, compassion, and meaning, all the things that make us human do not matter as long as we can cope and function. Whether we acknowledge it or not, we seem to look at people as 'human doings', or 'human functionings', not human *beings*.

This approach to life and to mental health is ignorant, uncaring and cruel. It is the same as what led the British military to execute soldiers with 'shellshock' for being 'cowards' and 'deserters' during WWI. The military did not care how soldiers felt, or what happened to them psychologically. All that mattered was that they continued to function. When they no longer could (because killing other humans is not something that healthy humans do easily, or without a heavy psychological and spiritual cost), they did not deserve to live anymore. They were nothing more than *objects* for a purpose. They were discarded just like a broken machine or gadget that can no longer be repaired.

A lot of people seek therapy, or are sent to see a therapist, only when they cannot function anymore. People begin to seek help when they have reached the limits of the resources that enable them to cope, or when the crutches they use become too toxic for them and those around them. No one comes to therapy when they still think they can cope.

Many view psychological difficulties as shameful, and asking for help as an admission of personal failure. It is hardly surprising in a society that evaluates people's worth and character by their ability to cope and function, regardless of anything.

I remember sitting through a module on career counselling back in the early days of my psychotherapy degree. The lecturer, a highly paid corporate psychologist, started by telling us that 95% of people work in jobs or occupations they do not care much about, that do not fulfil them, and are therefore miserable. Only 5%, he said, were among those fortunate enough to earn a living doing something they felt passionate about, and that meant something to them.

I expected the next sentence to be something about how our job as therapists would be to help those in the 95% group join the happier, more fulfilled 5%. Shockingly, he told us that our job was in fact to help the unhappy 95% continue to cope with their unfulfilled lives. He said this was 'just how things were in the world', and that it was 'unrealistic' to expect anything else.

As a new psychotherapy student, who had to work full time in order to pay for my studies, I was a member of the 95%. I had an admin assistant job that paid the bills, but a dream to open my own psychotherapy practice one day. Here was an 'expert' telling me that I was 'unrealistic', practically delusional. Those of us who were members of the 95% needed to let go of our naïve hopes or aspirations, because our chances of succeeding were slim.

This lecturer worked for wealthy corporations, and was paid big money to provide psychological services to their staff. His job was to offer them 'strategies' to cope with unfulfilling jobs in often unhealthy, uncaring, sometimes even abusive workplaces. The employers who paid his fees were his real clients, not the people who came to him for help.

Employee Assistance Programmes (EAP) can, and do offer limited short-term help. Who would not feel a little better when someone gives them undivided attention, and listens for a whole hour? But the purpose of psychological services like EAP, or the NHS is to restore people to functioning. From a symptom-management, coping-focused perspective, people's history, or the circumstances of their lives do not matter. Who they are as people, does not matter.

I have been increasingly disappointed with the way my profession has colluded with our economics, and our utilitarian approach to people. What passes as therapy these days[2] is often little more than a sticking plaster. It is not easy to be in private practice, and not every practitioner wants to be self-employed. In order to make a living, many practitioners are forced to compromise their principles. They are expected to deliver 'therapies' they do not believe in, and that offer little value to their clients. How can professionals who are forced to compromise for a living, support clients who yearn to stop compromising?

Since its advent in the 1940s, and for the following three decades, humanistic psychology revolutionised mental health services. It was a necessary reaction against the medical model, and the bleakness of psychoanalysis, and behaviourism that dominated mental health services.

When neoliberalist economics began to tighten its grip on the Western world in the 1980s, the great achievements of humanistic psychology were rapidly scaled back. Mental health services are once again obsessed with symptoms, and symptom-management, and human mental health is more medicalised than ever.

Nothing in nature, including us, can thrive without the right conditions and ingredients. By 'thrive' I mean become all that the plant or creature is capable of becoming – not just stay alive. Life (we do not know what life really is) seems quite resilient. Even in dismal conditions life always tries to continue. Scientists keep discovering life in the most inhospitable, and unlikely places on Earth. Survival is one thing. But whether a plant or creature will thrive is a different story.

Carl Rogers was from a farming family. Already as a child he realised that everything in nature needs the right conditions to thrive:

"I remember that in my boyhood, the bin in which we stored our winter's supply of potatoes was in the basement, several feet below a small window. The conditions were unfavourable, but the potatoes would begin to sprout—pale white sprouts, so unlike the healthy green shoots they sent up when planted in the soil in the spring. But these sad, spindly sprouts would grow 2 or 3 feet in length as they reached towards the distant light of the window. … They would never become plants, never mature, never fulfill

---

[2] There are, of course, many good therapists who do great work and who also try to make a difference to society. But I believe they are the exception not the rule.

their real potential. But under the most adverse circumstances, they were striving to become. Life would not give up, even if it could not flourish. In dealing with clients whose lives have been terribly warped, in working with men and women in the back wards of state hospitals, I often think of those potato sprouts. So unfavourable have been the conditions in which these people have developed that their lives often seem abnormal, twisted, scarcely human. Yet the directional tendency in them can be trusted. The clue to understanding their behavior is that they are striving in the only ways that they perceive as available to them, to move toward growth, toward becoming. To healthy persons, the results may seem bizarre and futile but they are life's desperate attempt to become itself."– Carl Rogers. (1980) *A Way of Being*. 1980. (pp118-119).

Farmers do not just throw seeds on the ground and hope for the best. They know how to give their crops the best conditions to develop to their full potential. If farmers operated their farms like we run societies, we would starve. Perhaps psychotherapy exists because we are starving psychologically and spiritually[3].

Try to criticise that unsuccessful plant in your garden that is not doing so well. *"Hey there raspberry! How dare you produce such poor and misshapen fruit? What is wrong with you? Get on with it! Life is what you make it, mate."* Try to tell the plant that it does not matter that you did not read the instructions, and planted it in the wrong position with insufficient sunlight, water, or nutrients. Tell your plant it should do just fine, *because,* well… why exactly?

I should not have to write this in 2023, but we seem to have forgotten that psychological difficulties are a direct result of a failure to grow. We have also forgotten that symptoms are not something to fight, or vanquish, but a pointer to where the real problem is.

No one does well when all they can look forward to is surviving from one day to the next. Coping can be necessary for a little while when life throws a curveball, but coping and mere existence are not life. All we need to do to reverse our mental health pandemic is start helping people

---

[3] There are millions of humans on the planet who are starving because they do not have enough food. They and their children do not even get the option of thinking about more than daily survival. This is inexcusable.

to grow towards their potential. A society that places the fulfilment of every person's potential at the centre of everything, will have no need for psychotherapy.

We already know all we need to know to raise young humans into whole, and thriving human beings who would not need therapy. But we seem determined to continue on our unhappy path, and choose leaders who keep us on it. We do not seem to have the will to offer the best conditions for everyone to develop to their full humanness.

The last three decades have seen significant progress in neuroscience and our understanding of psychology. One of the most revolutionary contributions comes from Dr Dan Siegel's framework of Interpersonal Neurobiology (IPNB). IPNB is a multidisciplinary way of thinking about what it means to be human. Among other things it brought the brain into psychotherapy. We already know that all learning requires brain systems to wire and connect. But prior to IPNB psychotherapy ignored the brain. IPNB reminds us of what should have been obvious, that there cannot be any significant or permanent change in our psychology without changes to brain connectivity.

The implications of IPNB for psychotherapy and mental health[4] are unprecedented, and have the power to transform the profession. IPNB is entirely compatible with humanistic and existential psychology, because it is about the process of becoming more fully what we are.

Over the years I have looked at everything I do in my therapy work. I got rid of practices or techniques of little value, and kept and developed others that make sense within the framework of IPNB. Therapy, especially for clients with trauma, is safer and more efficient. It is also exciting, inspiring, rich, warm, and full of life.

In line with the principles of humanistic psychology, clients are truly empowered. They know exactly what they are doing in therapy, and they are in charge of the therapeutic process. My clients do not suffer in therapy, they enjoy it, and so do I. No matter how difficult people's stories are, there is nothing more joyful than seeing a person rewire what their past wired into their brain, and become more and more who they were always meant to be. Therapy is a process that restores people back on the path towards optimal development; the path they would

---

[4] As well as for parenting and education

have been on if everything in their childhood and throughout life supported their growth.

This book explains why we are caught between surviving and thriving, and why we are so biased in favour of coping and survival. Most people have no idea what psychotherapy is, or what it can offer them. In this book I aim to take all the mystery out of mental health and therapy, and I share everything I do with my clients. The benefits extend far beyond the individual to everyone in their life, especially children and young people.

In this book I share exactly what we need to do to move towards fulfilling our potential as individuals, and as societies. As my clients can testify, it is simpler than you imagine (I said simple, not easy). It costs nothing, it is based on mainstream neuroscience, it confirms what we all know instinctively that is good for us, and it is at everyone's fingertips.

Like all professionals, therapists have to work within the boundaries of their training, and what they know they can offer. I do not work with people who have mental health diagnoses such as personality disorders, psychosis, bi-polar disorder, or schizophrenia. This is because I do not know how the work I do might impact on people with those conditions.

I also do not see people who are actively drinking or abusing drugs, or who are in serious crisis. If people do have a history of drug and/or alcohol use, they need to be completely clean for at least a year, committed to recovery, and have a well-established support network in place, before I can accept them for therapy. A therapist in private practice cannot provide crisis support, and cannot provide the ongoing, close support needed when people are just starting on a journey to recover from an addiction. For therapy to work, people's brains need to be in good condition. I ask my clients to stop drinking alcohol completely. Alcohol disables the most important parts of the brain that we need in order to grow and develop.

Nothing in this book is harmful. But if you do have a serious condition, you need to make sure you see someone who can offer the right kind of help, and not try to deal with it on your own. If you have a history of childhood trauma it is also important that you seek an appropriately trained professional who can offer you the help and support you need.

Despite what neoliberalist psychology tries to make people believe, our individual happiness and wellbeing cannot exist in isolation from our relationships. Each of us has an impact on what our groups and societies feel like to live in, the 'atmosphere' within them. We are each responsible for how our societies function, what they value, how they choose to distribute resources, how they look after our physical environment, how they treat individuals, and the kind of leaders they choose.

In turn, the societies we are born into determine how we each develop, the resources we have access to, the nature of our physical and relational environments, and what opportunities are available to us. Our societies can either contribute to our individual growth and development, or move us away from them by forcing us to spend too much of our time and mental resources on just coping and enduring.

As each of us moves towards fulfilling our potential, and being well, we interact with others differently. As we change, we have a positive impact on everyone around us, not just by what we consciously do or say, but by our very presence.

This is why this book is not just for individuals. The knowledge we have that I share in this book carries the potential to change us as a species. This book is for people who want to grow not just for themselves, but because they want to have a positive impact on their environment.

The reason I feel confident enough to share my work in a book is not because I know everything. But because I am privileged to witness profound transformations right before my eyes as a matter of routine. I receive ongoing feedback from all my clients that what we do in therapy is life-changing beyond anything they could have anticipated. In fact, this book exists because many clients urged me to write up my work and make it available to everyone.

People tend to reach out to self-help literature usually during difficult times. They might not have the 'brain space' to concentrate on long books. I therefore keep the publications in this series as short as possible.

The feedback I receive has consistently validated this decision. To keep my books short, I do have to leave things out. But I include everything I think is important. I aim to communicate in a clear and focused way, so that readers can make the most out of the time they invest in reading.

Each chapter in this book builds on the previous ones. If you read the chapters in order, they will reflect the coherent framework I am trying to communicate. I repeat key concepts in a few places for the benefit of those who choose to read in a less structured way.

I have re-written and expanded the section on feelings/emotions for this edition. In response to suggestions from fellow practitioners who use my books with their clients, the new and expanded chapter now includes relevant material from my book on anxiety.

I have recently created a journal/workbook designed specifically to accompany this book. I called it, *Let's Integrate. Your journal/workbook companion to Therapy Without A Therapist*. It can help in staying on track the work of integration that I share and teach in this book. *Let's Integrate* is available in paperback and hardcover formats on Amazon worldwide.

We are a sophisticated species with enormous potential. We have an untapped capacity to create a kind and safe growth-focused world where monetisation, hoarding, and rationing, especially of essential resources, would not be necessary. I would like to live in a world where all knowledge is freely available to everyone. In the world we live in now, I charge for my work in order to make a living, and you had to pay for this book. I apologise.

As always, I encourage you to read critically, question what I write, and use as many resources as you can to help you on your journey.

Thank you for your dedication to your growth and development. By investing in your own growth, you make the world a better place. I welcome feedback. You can contact me through my website, fullyhuman.co.uk, or via my Substack page, 'Fully Human Essays'.

Avigail Abarbanel
Scottish Highlands
August 2023

What is Therapy Really?...

Even for people who are open minded, the field of mental health can be intimidating. Most people have no idea what psychotherapy is or what therapists do and I do not think this is acceptable. You can live a perfectly good life without understanding the first thing about quantum physics or how a washing machine works but mental health is everyone's business.

What we call 'mental health' (and much of the knowledge and practice we have around it) is at the very centre of what we are and how we operate as individuals, families, groups and societies. I believe that it is not OK for this kind of knowledge to be the exclusive domain of a separate and 'mysterious' field, left only to 'experts'.

I think most therapists communicate what they do in a language that is too vague. TV and movies are also not much help. They do not often give an accurate picture of what therapy is. Script writers show therapy the way they imagine it, which is often just as 'mysterious' and unclear as it appears anyway.

I think that when people ask for help with their mental health, they should know exactly what to ask for and understand what they are offered. I also think people should feel like they can make informed choices about the kind of psychological help they get. But it can be hard to make good choices in any area where you do not know enough.

Why things are this way is a topic that would need a book in its own right. But in short, up until the last decade and a half or so, the profession of psychotherapy has not been particularly clear about what exactly it is doing and how it is helping people (or not). Thankfully, things have been changing. There is no longer an excuse for therapists to be vague. We can and should be able to explain to everyone in a clear way what we do in therapy and how therapy is supposed to work.

Is Therapy About Talking?

It is a common perception that talking to someone can be helpful. Just talking and having a good listener who can make you feel understood and accepted without judgement is assumed to be immensely helpful. People often feel better when they have a chance to 'offload' and 'get things off their chest'. But what does 'helpful' mean? What does it mean to feel 'better' and how long does it last? What kind of 'talking' are we talking about? Is talking to someone 'therapy' and… is it for everyone?

Over the past two decades I have heard from many people that, sometimes, talking to therapists has made things worse, not better. They have brought up things that were painful or disturbing and ended up with an open 'can of worms' they didn't know what to do with.

I have heard many stories about therapy sessions ending while people were in tears and in 'bits' but they had to leave the room, because 'time was up'. Others have said their therapists were too quiet and said little or nothing throughout the whole session, which made them feel 'weird' and uncomfortable. Some people have said that therapists told them obvious things they already knew or that they could easily find in a book. Even people who have been helped by therapy up to a point have said that after a few sessions they felt they 'ran out of things to talk about' and didn't feel that they were 'getting anywhere' anymore.

Some clients have told me that when they felt strong emotions and wanted to talk to previous therapists about painful things, they were actively prevented from expressing emotions. Others felt they were pushed too far when they were not ready. A small number of people I have spoken to, who were a little more confident and have questioned their therapist or the therapy, have indicated (usually apologetically) that they felt the therapist was less intelligent than them, or they felt the therapist did not seem to understand them. Recently a client told me that when she asked her previous therapist (in private practice) to explain how he works, he became defensive and refused to answer. Instead of responding to a perfectly fair question, the therapist saw the client's question as a personal affront or a challenge.

Therapy that doesn't help is not just useless or a waste of time or money. It can be, and often is, indirectly harmful. That's because most people tend to blame themselves when therapy doesn't work for them. They assume that therapists know what they are doing. So, if talking to a therapist hasn't helped or hasn't helped much, they think that their problems are too complicated or 'unfixable'. This can leave people feeling hopeless that positive change might be possible. Many can cope with this, but for some this can be devastating.

Carl Rogers, the great humanistic psychologist and the creator of person-centred psychotherapy, believed that talking to an empathetic, non-judgemental and congruent (genuine) therapist, should be enough to help people change. While a small minority of non-traumatised clients can change through such an encounter, the reality is that it is not enough for the majority of people. Talking in such an environment can help people feel better. Sometimes sharing a secret or a shameful thought or feeling, an inner conflict, with a trusted and non-judgemental therapist can be a great relief. But does this experience change us forever? Not necessarily.

There is also a real risk of clients developing dependency. As the famous psychologist Carl Jung rightly said, "a favourable environment merely strengthens the dangerous tendency to expect everything to originate from the outside..." (*The Undiscovered Self.* p.58). Clients are likely to feel safer and more comfortable in the company of a caring and warm therapist. They might 'bask in the glow' of the experience for a few days after the session. But what happens next? If clients come to therapy because it is the only place where they can find unconditional acceptance and empathy, there is a risk that therapy will be nothing more than a 'feel good pill'.

Counselling or Psychotherapy?

In my past, before I became a therapist, I experienced 'therapy' that felt like it hurt me more than it helped. How do you know if the hurt or discomfort you might feel in therapy is a natural part of the process, or a sign that your mind is being mishandled or harmed? People often do not know, especially if they are in a vulnerable state and are desperate for help. On a few occasions in my history, I felt more traumatised than helped by the 'therapy' I had. At the time I did not understand why this happened. Like many, I thought it was because I was 'too damaged' and 'beyond help'.

One therapist, a psychologist whom I saw briefly in my twenties, set me back years from facing my history of sexual abuse by telling me, without any basis, that it couldn't have happened. Like many adult victims of childhood abuse there was something in me that didn't want to accept what was done to me. This part of me wanted to believe the therapist. I was also young and I lacked confidence. I trusted the therapist and saw him as a knowledgeable authority figure. What he said carried a lot of weight at the time. But it was wrong and clumsy and in hindsight I realised that it set me back years in my recovery.

One of the reasons that I sometimes felt more harmed than helped was because the approaches I encountered were not what I needed. Another reason was that therapists did not have the skill or knowledge to offer me what I needed. At the time, I did not have any understanding and had assumed that all therapists worked the same way and did the same thing.

I remember a particularly bad 'therapy' experience in my late twenties at my university in Sydney. I was going through a difficult time and felt like I couldn't cope. I was chronically anxious and extremely stressed, even more than usual. Although I was an intelligent and capable twenty-seven-year-old, I felt I could not manage my life. Reluctantly and apprehensively I decided to 'take responsibility' and made an appointment with the student counsellor on campus. The counsellor was a qualified professional with a Master's degree in Psychology. When I walked in I was as nervous as hell. I had no idea what I was supposed to do or how to 'be a client'.

As I walked into the room it felt almost immediately like there wasn't a lot of warmth there. The therapist seemed tired, bored and uninterested but I pushed my first impressions aside. I always did that because I had no confidence and didn't trust myself or my 'gut feeling' about anything, especially people. I also didn't want to be judgemental, even in my own head. I was so desperate for some kind of help that I needed to believe it was available.

At that time, I didn't know that I suffered from severe post-traumatic stress because of a horrifically abusive childhood that I hadn't begun to acknowledge. Like most victims of childhood trauma, I was anxious and nervous almost all the time. I was scared and also ashamed to walk into the office of a mental health professional. I was in a vulnerable psychological state anyway, but facing a stranger and admitting that I couldn't manage my life and that I needed help made me feel much worse.

When the psychologist asked me what I came to see her for, I tried to explain that I was feeling stressed and worried all the time and that I wasn't managing my life and my studies. I didn't get far when she stopped me and told me that I needed to relax. (The last thing I was able to do was to relax[5]. If I had been able to relax I would not have needed to see a therapist in the first place). She then said she wanted to teach me a relaxation exercise and explained that this was how we were going to use the session.

I tried to tell her that I didn't think this was what I needed, but I didn't quite know how to say it and there was no negotiating with her. She was in charge and nothing I said made any difference, which interestingly, is exactly what my childhood had been like. I had never been listened to, or taken seriously and was not allowed to question or refuse authority figures. Here I was, in 'therapy', experiencing the same thing. Because I perceived the therapist to be in charge, I pushed my feelings aside and tried to do what she asked. When I tried to follow her instructions and engage in the relaxation exercise, I became even more nervous and started to feel panicked. Somehow, I found the strength to stop. I mumbled something about it not helping and ran out of the room. I didn't make another appointment.

I remember leaving that session feeling even more hopeless, ashamed and scared than when I walked in. I felt like a failure. I worried that I had offended the therapist and worried even more than usual that there was no help for me. I then 'picked myself up' and told myself to 'get on with it' as I always did anyway. I told myself I would have to continue to keep coping on my own. I remember feeling very frightened.

If the therapist had taken the time to interact with me, she would have realised two important things. Firstly, that I was suffering from the impact of severe childhood trauma and that I needed skilled, *long-term* psychotherapy. She would have known that, as a trauma victim, there was no way that I could relax, let alone attempt this in front of someone I had just met. And secondly, that I was a new immigrant to Australia. I was financially and socially insecure and I was still adjusting to a massive life change.

---

[5] A well-informed therapist would know that a traumatised brain would naturally resist any attempts to relax it. It is like saying to someone who is facing a ferocious bear that they should just chill. Trauma makes people feel like they are facing an immediate mortal threat to their survival almost all of the time. The last thing people need is to be told to relax because it is asking them to drop their guard. Dropping our guard is too risky when facing a mortal threat. This is why many traumatised people avoid mindfulness exercises or feel panicked when they try to relax, do breathing exercises or meditate. (See my booklet on trauma in this series).

Adjustment to a major life change on top of childhood trauma is challenging and frightening. It would have helped me immensely if the psychologist had just explained that I was adjusting to a big life change and that it was *normal* to feel more stressed and insecure than usual. This would have left me with a bit of reassurance that, given the circumstances, my feelings were normal and that I was not going crazy. I could have been spared some of the sense of failure and shame I felt about feeling bad and not coping. There is a good chance that I would have experienced the therapist as understanding and caring and as *interested* and I would have trusted her enough to come back.

But that therapist was trained in using and teaching *strategies* to help people *manage symptoms*. She was not trained in long-term, developmental psychotherapy. She thought her role was to try and help me *feel better* so that I could *cope* or function better. She did not take the time to find out about me, my background and present life circumstances because it was not required by the symptom-management approach (or 'modality') she was practicing[6].

The therapist asked me why I came to see her. But she didn't ask what I wanted or hoped for from therapy. I didn't know what to ask for because I didn't know what therapy was. I felt like a mess anyway, as many of my own clients often feel in the first session. I didn't have the presence of mind to ask even if I knew what to ask. I didn't know that the therapist's attempt to teach me a relaxation technique was, in fact, 'counselling', not 'psychotherapy'. I did not know anything about either and was not given a choice.

My professional association, the BACP (British Association of Counselling and Psychotherapy) has been grappling with the task of defining 'counselling' and 'psychotherapy', deciding what kind of training each should require and how we should explain it all to the public. I do not know yet what the outcome of this process will be. But in my work, I have always been clear about the difference between 'counselling' and 'psychotherapy'. I have always relied on a useful definition from my training back in Australia. According to that definition, counselling is there to help with more surface issues, while psychotherapy is about 'characterological' changes.

---

[6] This counsellor's approach was very likely based on CBT – Cognitive Behavioural Therapy. Psychologists in Australia are trained to believe that CBT is the *only* approach that works in mental health.

Characterological changes are changes to the foundations of what makes us who we are. Unlike counselling, where you deal with one issue at a time (e.g., do breathing or relaxation exercises to manage stress, or try to control or manage debilitating anxiety to prepare for an upcoming presentation or assignment) psychotherapy changes us in a way that enables us to engage *differently* with whatever life throws at us. We change in how we approach life, how we react to things and how we see and understand ourselves and our reality. Counselling might help us change how we approach one issue, but psychotherapy changes us in a way that affects everything in our lives because it affects the very foundation of what makes us who we are.

Another clear distinction that I make between counselling and psychotherapy is that counselling is more about coping and functioning whereas psychotherapy is about development. Good quality psychotherapy can help people get back onto the original path to developing their potential; the path they would have been on if their childhood and life circumstances were ideal. When people begin to develop again, their symptoms tend to disappear naturally.

The different modalities or approaches to therapy that people are likely to encounter can be roughly divided between counselling and psychotherapy. We can tell the difference between them by looking at what they say about the purpose of therapy, and by what they say they can help people with.

For example, approaches like CBT (Cognitive Behaviour Therapy) are there, by their own definition, for 'symptom reduction', not for growth or development. Therefore, CBT can be seen as *counselling*, not as psychotherapy. Approaches such as Person-Centred Therapy, Gestalt Therapy, Psychodrama, Transactional Analysis (TA), Art Therapy, Jungian Therapy, Psychoanalytic/Psychodynamic therapy, Existential Therapy, each in their own way are intended to support people's development and are, therefore, *psychotherapy* approaches.

Psychiatrists, who are doctors with a speciality in mental health, rely on the 'medical model'. Psychiatrists diagnose mental/psychological 'disorders'[7] and offer whatever treatment might be available for that

---

[7] There is a lot of justified controversy about what is actually a 'disorder' in mental health and what is not. There has been fair criticism of psychiatry over many decades coming from different circles. For example, psychiatry has been slow and reluctant to acknowledge the damage that sexual abuse – they used to call it 'incest' – did to girls and women in particular. Psychiatry is guilty for setting us back decades in dealing with the sexual abuse of children as a society. Over the last

disorder, usually medication. (Not many psychiatrists in the UK are trained in psychotherapy or work as psychotherapists). At our current level of knowledge, medication does not cure mental disorders. It is therefore possible to see medication as a kind of 'counselling' because it is intended to help to reduce or manage symptoms. Sometimes medication can help to reduce severe symptoms in a way that enables people to engage with psychotherapy. I am therefore not dismissing medication and the role that it can play for some people.

Most of the clients I have met over the years who have been on antidepressants, have chosen to stop taking them within two to four months of starting therapy[8]. Many of my clients tell me in the first session that they are not happy to be reliant on pills (even if they do not suffer any serious side effects) and that they want to be well without them. They hope psychotherapy will help them live a full life without needing to use medication to regulate their emotions or mental states.

As a psychotherapy practitioner, I rarely offer counselling, but it doesn't mean that I do not see the value in it. I do, however, believe that people *need to know* if what they are getting is counselling or psychotherapy, so that they can make an informed choice. I am concerned that if everyone is offered only (or mostly) counselling, the message it sends to people is that managing symptoms is the best they can hope for.

In my life I never just wanted to cope. I wanted to live a full life. As a professional and a member of society I am interested in each and every one of us moving towards developing our potential, whatever it might be. Coping is what we are supposed to do for a little while, if

---

few decades psychiatry has been criticised for its tendency to over-diagnose mental illness and mental health issues, particularly in women. Psychiatry ignored the reality that women have for generations been discriminated against in society, that they were mostly powerless, that many women were victims of domestic and sexual abuse for generations, a fact ignored by society, and that they did not have the same opportunities as males to develop. This book is too short to go into this topic in any detail, but there is plenty of literature about it if you are interested. I believe psychiatry does have a valuable role to play in mental health and in society, and thankfully things are far better now than they used to be.

[8] Antidepressants are addictive, and people who decide to stop taking them do not always realise how severe the withdrawal symptoms can be. When people try to stop taking medication, the withdrawal symptoms can make them think that stopping was a mistake. If people decide to stop taking antidepressants it is important to do this very gradually and in consultation with a doctor, ideally one who knows their medical history and who has prescribed the medication. If people stop slowly enough – the slower the better – it allows their brain to get used to being without the drugs and the withdrawal symptoms tend to be much less dramatic.

circumstances are tough. The truth is that most people are already quite good at coping. There is little that counselling can teach people that they are not already doing themselves. Psychotherapy however, when practised properly, can be, and often is, a gamechanger.

A Gamechanger

In this book I aim to go to the very foundations of what we think of as mental health and psychotherapy, regardless of approach. If psychotherapy is about a real and permanent change in us, about growth and development, then we have to ask what these changes mean.

Everyone who comes to therapy wants something to change. But what does it mean to change in such a way that we feel more peaceful internally, have a better sense of self, feel more confident and grounded, more mature, more fulfilled, feel better about ourselves, others and life in general, are less prone to triggers, flow better with life and handle its demands with more ease and with a sense of purpose or have a better sense of direction in life? What is it exactly that changes in us when we no longer live with anxiety or stress?

In my profession, or even in pop-psychology, we use words and phrases like 'dealing with unfinished business', 'growing', 'developing', 'healing', 'resolving', 'becoming mature', 'getting closure', 'dealing with things', 'sorting'. But what does it mean and how does it happen? *Where* does this change happen?

The language that has traditionally been used in psychotherapy has not been helpful in clarifying, explaining or communicating to most people what mental health is or what psychotherapy does. In fact, I think it might have done the opposite, which is why so many people think that psychology and psychotherapy are either 'airy fairy' or intimidating.

Thanks to the revolutionary work of Dr Daniel Siegel, the developer of Interpersonal Neurobiology (IPNB), we are much clearer about what psychotherapy does, what it means to be psychologically, well and what it means to change or to grow. Dr Siegel's work has been a total gamechanger in the field of psychotherapy. It is now possible for therapists to understand what they are doing, and to explain to clients from all walks of life, what therapy is and how it is supposed to work for them.

IPNB has made us see more clearly, and acknowledge that any significant change to how we are, how we think, feel, behave, interact with others, what we believe about ourselves, others and the world, even how we move, depends on changes in the way our brain is wired. If we are different now to how we were before, it means that something in has changed in the 'architecture' of our brain.

Explaining key points about the brain and brain development and what therapy means in those terms, forms a part of the therapy process. If clients understand how our work together will help change their brain; if they are clear about what they are supposed to do in therapy to achieve this; if they know why and how their brain needs to change so that they can resolve the problems that brought them to therapy, they can be more actively in charge of their therapy process. Therapy doesn't have to continue to be a mystery. Therapists do not have to remain mysterious, 'airy fairy' or intimidating authority figures with a monopoly on psychological knowledge.

The brain is the hub of the human nervous system, which is distributed all over the body. Siegel calls it the 'embodied brain' to emphasise the fact that the brain is not just in the skull. But inside our skull is where everything is regulated and processed. The brain inside our skull is busy sending and receiving information to and from all parts of the nervous system throughout the body as well as to and from our environment, which includes other people.

Our brain enables us to do everything we do, know everything we know, be what we are and continually change and learn new things. Given the right conditions, it will also enable us to feel like we are growing towards our potential. The way the brain in the skull is wired, has a significant impact on everything we are because it determines how well information will be transferred and processed.

When you learn a new language or skill, you change something in your brain. As you engage with the learning process and practise the new skill, which usually means a lot of repetition, you create new neural pathways and new neural networks that 'contain' and enable the new language or skill. Repetition reinforces the connections until they become permanent. *Everything* we learn, *all learning*, is possible because of changes to our physical brain. Psychotherapy is no different. It is very real and very physical and everyone can understand it.

Different parts of the brain have specialities that enable us to do what we do and know what we know. For example, there are brain areas for hearing, sight, speaking, moving, for mathematical analysis and for all the richness of our human abilities and functions. The parts of the brain we need to connect for what we call growth and development, for better mental health or for fulfilling our potential, are different to those we need to connect in order to learn a language for example, or learn a new dance movement. But the process underneath, of connecting neurons and turning them into permanent neural networks that fire reliably and effortlessly is fundamentally the same.

IPNB is a multidisciplinary framework. It learns from many fields and honours many 'ways of knowing'. It puts what we know together in a way that enables us to practise therapy like never before. IPNB is also directly relevant to parenting and education. It is well grounded in science and it helps us understand properly what we think of as mental health, what it means to be human, how relationships play a part in our development and why or how we do well or not so well.

It is called '*Interpersonal* Neurobiology' to emphasise the fact that our neurobiology is not limited to what is happening inside each one of us. Our neurobiology is interconnected with our relationships. Psychotherapeutic frameworks like Gestalt therapy, argued decades ago that there is no self without relationships. This is why in Gestalt therapy there is such an emphasis on relationships: between the therapist and the client, in the client's life outside therapy and the internal relationship between different aspects of the client. The developers of Gestalt therapy concluded this from decades of study and observations of human beings, how they are in themselves and how they interact in relationships. Thanks to IPNB we now have the neuroscience to back this up.

You can think of my therapy work as 'applied IPNB'. I have had many years to study and understand how different therapy approaches work (or not) from an IPNB perspective and to adjust the way I work accordingly. I have 'cleaned up' my practice by getting rid of techniques or approaches that do not work or that are a bit of a waste of time. I have kept and developed what works more effectively and efficiently.

A good therapist is supposed to be a skilled *facilitator,* a skilled *companion* and an *ally* through the therapeutic journey. These ideas are not new. What is new is thinking of ourselves as people who facilitate and support the process of our clients actively changing the wiring of their brains. In my initial training the brain did not feature at all, which is partly what made therapy seem a bit vague. Thankfully things have now changed.

As far as I am concerned, mental health is too important to leave it to chance and guesswork. We each have a limited time on Earth. As a practitioner, I feel a duty to make sure every moment of my clients' time in therapy and every penny they pay me count. IPNB has made this more possible than ever before.

Not One Brain, Three!

Working from within the framework of Interpersonal Neurobiology (IPNB) therapists are encouraged to explain the brain to clients. This is usually what I do in the first session with every new client (I call it 'the brain lecture').

Clients need to understand their brain, in particular those aspects about it that are relevant to mental health and therapy. This enables them to understand what we are supposed to be doing in therapy and how it can address their concerns. They then understand better what my therapeutic role is and what they are there to do in therapy. This enables them to become clearer about what it is they are after and make an informed choice about whether or not they wish to work with me.

Once clients understand the framework I work from, they can feel more in charge of their therapy, which they no longer see as mysterious, 'airy fairy' or threatening. It also relieves any shame about 'failures', 'character flaws' or 'weaknesses', or any embarrassment about seeking help. People's dignity is preserved once they understand that they are not broken and that I am not there to 'fix' them (as if I could...). When people understand what is going on in their brain and how it has been affected (wired) by their life experiences, they realise their problems are not 'their fault'. They are not stupid, bad, weak or difficult, but like everyone else they are a product of their environment and circumstances. Another thing that is removed is blame, both of self and of parents or others.

The 'Brain Lecture'...

You do not need to become a neuroscientist to know just enough about the brain to understand what therapy is about and learn the practices you need in order to change in significant ways.

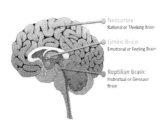

I usually start by asking what might sound like a silly question: *How many brains do we have?* The chapter heading already gave it away, so yes, we do have three brains, not one and they are each divided between our two hemispheres.

The 'Triune (three) Brain Model' was developed by the neuroscientist Paul MacLean in the 1960s. Our three brains, seem to reflect the stages of evolution of life on this planet: from reptile to mammal and then to human, a uniquely complex and self-aware mammal. Each of our brains has evolved to handle increasingly complex tasks.

MacLean believed that our three brains have different 'mentalities' and he thought that they are not necessarily linked together or 'talk to each other' as well as they could. Once you read about the different brains and refer to your own experience, especially how you relate to others and how you behave in situations when you feel under threat, you'll realise MacLean made a good point.

The Reptilian Brain

If your reptilian brain (also called the 'cerebellum' or 'brain stem') is working the way it is supposed to, then you are alive and breathing. The reptilian brain is the 'command centre' for all of our automatic (autonomic) physical functions. Everything that keeps our bodies going automatically and that ticks along on its own in the background is regulated in this brain. Functions such as our immune system, digestion, blood pressure, heartbeat or breathing, are all regulated by the reptilian brain.

Damage to this brain can be, and often is, disastrous because it can cause some or all of the autonomic functions to stop. When the cerebellum is badly damaged in a car crash for example, people can go into a 'vegetative' state and sometimes machines are needed to keep their bodies going. That's because the body is no longer able to perform on its own the tasks needed to support its continued functioning and survival.

I often joke with my clients that if they are alive and breathing in front of me, it means that their reptilian brain is working, so we do not need to worry about it so much in therapy. It's the next two brains that are much more significant in our work.

The Limbic (Mammal) Brain

The limbic brain or system is our mammalian brain. It sits on top of the reptilian brain and is located in the middle of our skull, divided between the two hemispheres. It is the brain we have in common with all other mammals on this planet. It is an ancient brain, and in different types of mammals it has different levels of complexity. In primates and in humans it is especially complex.

If the limbic brain has an 'agenda', 'job' or 'purpose' it is the *survival of our species*. It's not 'interested' if, as individuals, we are happy or not, good or bad, if our life is particularly fulfilling, happy or satisfying. Our limbic brain works in the service of nature. It 'cares' only that we survive long enough to have children, protect them for as long as necessary until they can survive on their own and have more children, all for the purpose of the continuation of our species.

If you think in terms of numbers, then the human limbic brain has so far done a great job. There are 7.8 billion humans on the planet and growing. We are the dominant species on this planet, the top predator and the species that, we think, has the most profound impact (for better or worse) on the natural environment and other species on Earth. It is our species that has changed this planet beyond recognition in a relatively short time.

The limbic system (working together with the reptilian brain) is responsible for triggering and regulating our 'fight'- 'flight'- 'freeze' responses. These are the ancient, hard-wired instinctual reactions to threat and danger that have helped our species survive so well on a hostile planet. It seems that the reptilian and mammalian brain are in constant communication. Information flows constantly from the entire nervous system through the spinal cord into the reptilian brain and from there up to the limbic brain system.

Our limbic brain uses our five senses to scan the inside of our body and our external environment constantly, to check if we are safe or not. If we face a threat, a part of the limbic brain called the amygdala 'sounds the alarm'. This triggers a cocktail of chemicals to flow into our blood and through the body so that different muscle groups and functions can be activated to enable the survival responses of fight, flight or freeze that have worked well for our species and have brought us to where we are today. These short-term responses are intended to ensure that we survive an immediate threat to live another day.

Our Ancient Survival Instincts

Fight

If we are supposed to fight off a threat, our survival chemicals (also called 'stress hormones') will make our upper body tense up, energise our muscles and prepare them for action. We will feel a surge of energy in our upper body as our arms get ready to push something or someone off, or to fight. When the 'fight' response is triggered, people often demonstrate several times their normal strength. When people get angry and feel the blood rush up to their heads and their upper body and the muscles of the upper body tense up, it's because this is exactly what happens.

A lot of people also feel hotter. Heat is the way we experience energy in the body. When someone gets angry, we might say they feel 'hot under the collar'. Anger is the emotion associated with the 'fight' response. It is part of the mechanism that activates our fight instinct and that gives our body the strength and energy to try to push away or fight off a threat. Aches and pains in the upper body, like neck or shoulder pain and tension headaches might have something to do with living with a lot of anger or recurring anger without realising it.

Flight

If the response our limbic brain chooses is to flee, the bottom half of the body will become activated, the muscles in the legs will tense up, ready to run. Our digestive system, which normally takes up a huge amount of energy (do you remember the last time you felt tired and sluggish after a particularly big meal?) will shut down temporarily and so will our immune system.

When you are facing an immediate threat, long-term functions such as digestion are not so important. The body automatically diverts energy from digestion or the immune system to ensure we have what we need to survive in the short-term. Once we survive the threat to live another day, our long-term functions will return to normal.

Another advantage of stopping or slowing down the digestive system is that our bowels and bladder will try to empty. A lot of people feel sick when they get scared and might vomit if their stomach has something in it. Running with an empty stomach, bowels and bladder makes us lighter on our feet and faster. More of our ancestors were able to flee more quickly when their bowels were emptied and chances of survival optimised. This is why this ability or instinct is still with us.

When people are afraid they can feel the blood drain out of their faces, or heads. They might feel a 'sinking' feeling in their guts, get a tummy ache, wind or diarrhoea or feel their legs shaking. All these symptoms reflect exactly what happens in the different systems of their body as it prepares for and adjusts quickly to the need to flee from danger.

Fear is the emotion associated with the flight (fleeing) response. It helps activate the instinct to escape a threat and energises the necessary parts of the body to help us run as quickly as possible. Problems like Irritable Bowel Syndrome (IBS) or restless legs for example, might well be a result of living in a chronic state of fear without realising it. As a traumatised child I grew up with IBS. It wasn't until I began to recover from my trauma, that this problem disappeared. Prior to my recovery I had no idea that you could go to the toilet without experiencing pain.

Freeze

Freezing – also called 'dorsal', or horizontal 'dive' – probably has a lot to do with 'playing dead'. When we cannot fight or flee, freeze might be the only option to try to stay alive. In freeze mode, the body will go into a mild shock-like state and will want to collapse so we will feel like we want to drop and lie down. Our bodily functions slow down and our skin feels cold to the touch to the point where we can appear dead. Some of our ancestors probably survived by appearing dead to potential predators who didn't like to eat dead things and preferred to kill their prey and consume it fresh. Enough of our ancestors survived thanks to this ability, which is why it is also still with us alongside the fight and fleeing responses.

Children who are attacked by or frightened of the people who are supposed to keep them safe, do not have the option to fight or to flee their caregivers. Children cannot fight an adult attacker and they cannot flee because they are too young to survive on their own. The only remaining option is to freeze. If this happens a lot in childhood, this response becomes reinforced and ends up hardwired into the brain we take with us into adult life. I believe this is the reason why many victims of abuse report experiencing what sounds like the freeze reaction when they feel under threat or have a flashback. A lot of victims of abuse describe feeling paralysed and unable to do anything whenever they feel threatened.

I have a strong suspicion that conditions like fibromyalgia or chronic fatigue have a lot to do with the freeze response. As someone who has suffered from fibromyalgia probably from my mid-teens right into my early thirties, I know what this can feel like. The body wants to collapse and drop and all our functions want to slow down, which makes the limbs feel like they are filled 'with lead'. Because we live in a world that can measure our worth by how well we function, we feel like we have to keep going and we might try to push through this. This can then lead to more exhaustion and to pain in the joints and the muscles. People who realise they have to take time out because of this can feel a lot of shame and a sense of failure. I have often wondered if the emotion that is associated with the 'freeze' response is a kind of numbness, something even beyond fear, a sense of 'giving up'.

Attachment

You might have heard the word 'attachment' used quite a lot in the past few years, especially in relation to raising children. The limbic brain enables mammals to bond with members of their own species (and of other species). This bond is what we call attachment and it is something that reptiles are not so good at. Those who developed attachment theory back in the 1940s noticed that if a reptile is frightened, it would run to a safe place. But if a young mammal is frightened it would tend to run to an older member of its own species for protection.

Attachment is the protective bond between adult mammals and their young. It enables and ensures the survival of the young. Attachment in humans can be 'secure' or 'insecure'. The type of attachment we are allowed to develop, or that is available to us after we are born has been found to have significant impact on the development of our brain. Most human parents are able to keep their children *alive* even when all they can offer is insecure attachment. But whether parents are able to help children develop into happy, healthy and fulfilled adults is a different matter.

Some mammals such as wolves, primates, whales or dolphins, for example, are able to cooperate and work together as groups. There are degrees of cooperation depending on the species. There are also social structures and rules that regulate how mammal groups function and how individuals in the group relate to each other and how they function in the group. The more advanced the species, the more complex the social structures and rules tend to be. All of this is always in the service of the survival of the species.

Mammals benefit from cooperation up to a point. Shortage of food and the presence of constant threat and danger do not necessarily bring out the 'best' (a human concept) in individual mammals. They would easily kill, abandon each other to die of hunger or be captured by a predator just to save themselves. They are not 'evil'. They do not do it 'deliberately'. This is just a result of the struggle to survive in an uncertain and dangerous environment. In humanity we see both cooperation and competition in threatening situations such as war or natural disasters, or when the normal structure of life suddenly breaks down and survival is no longer guaranteed.

Those who survive longer get to pass on their genes to the next generation. Those who die before they have a chance to have children, do not. In the dangerous world we come from, the stronger, more aggressive or cunning individuals probably survived longer. It is their genes, including the genes responsible for cunning, ruthlessness or aggression that would then be passed on generationally. When the environment changes in a significant way and certain abilities or qualities no longer help a species survive, the species will either reduce in numbers or become extinct. If there is enough time, the species might evolve to adapt to the new conditions in order to continue to survive. Human beings also have the ability to cooperate and sacrifice ourselves for others. In some situations, these abilities helped our ancestors survive better. They were therefore passed on genetically through our evolution.

Our strongest and most significant attachment to other people, things or places is directly related to our survival. Safety is the key to survival, so we develop the strongest attachment where our limbic brain instinctively perceives that we are safest (not necessarily happiest or most fulfilled). Social workers who work in child protection and have the difficult task of removing children from their families when they are victims of abuse, are familiar with the phenomenon of abused children clinging to abusive adults and refusing to be taken away. Some people have misinterpreted this to mean that things might not be 'as bad' for these children as previously assumed, despite evidence to the contrary. No matter how much a child is suffering, their limbic brain tells them they are safer in the place they know with the people they know, and are not safe going away with a stranger into the unknown. A similar thing can happen when women who are victims of domestic abuse refuse to leave an abusive relationship, despite the fact that it is harmful and dangerous. What we are attached to is what we consider familiar and, therefore, safe. The new and unfamiliar, that which we do not yet have an attachment to, is automatically perceived as threatening.

> ## From a limbic perspective
>
> Attachment = Familiarity
> Familiar = Safe
> Unfamiliar = Danger/threat

Human children are vulnerable for a lot longer than the young of other mammals. It takes a long time before young humans are ready to survive on their own. Regardless of whether the environment is safe or unsafe *psychologically*, we still depend on it for our *physical* survival. We have no choice about this because physical survival takes priority over everything else.

Even in adult relationships, attachment plays an enormous part and is strongly linked to survival. When people fall in love, or when they have been together for a long time, their limbic brain believes that their life depends on their partner (in the same way that, historically, survival depended on their parents or care givers). When someone close dies, it is normal for those who were closely attached to them to feel, at least in the beginning, as if they could not survive without them, although logically they know that they can.

Letting go of a relationship that's over, or grieving over losing someone, is a process of rewiring attachment. It is where we gradually sever our attachment, 'un-attaching' ourselves from the person we used to be attached to. Severing attachment is one of the most painful and scary things anyone ever has to go through. It is always worse when it is forced on us by betrayal, death or other circumstances beyond our control. We also develop attachment to objects, places or roles we have held. This is why people grieve (rewire their attachment) when they move, change jobs, retire or lose an object that is significance for them.

A Fear-Based Brain

Anyone who criticises other people for feeling fear may not understand how we are made. Our limbic brain is *fear-based* because we have evolved on a harsh and dangerous planet where survival was not guaranteed. Our ancestors, with brains just like ours, were still competing with dangerous predators for food and territory. Studies that looked at the DNA of fossilised remains of large predators, discovered that we were a significant source of food for those dangerous and powerful animals. In other words, our ancestors had good reasons to be frightened. Being fearful helped us survive better. If you are afraid, you are more likely to be careful and watchful and not take unnecessary risks.

Our limbic brain is primed for and is *fine-tuned* to fear. From the moment we are born our limbic brain begins to wire in a catalogue of all the things we should be afraid of and worry about. Everything that's ever happened to us, everything we have experienced, is wired into our limbic system, *especially* if it was significant to our survival and was associated with fear or threat.

Children who have little life experience naturally look to adults who are more experienced to help them learn and adapt to the environment they are born into so that they can survive. At the start of life, and for quite a few years after, we depend on the environment around us and the adults who look after us to guide and teach us what we should or shouldn't worry about.

Children are filled with fears and their fears should always be taken seriously. Children whose fears are not taken seriously tend to grow up into adults who suffer from chronic fears ('anxiety'). An adult's 'job' is to teach children which things are worth worrying about and what things are not such a big problem. (Is dropping and breaking a glass of milk on the same level of significance as crossing the road without looking?) Helping children with their fears has to be done sensitively and skilfully. Dismissing fears, belittling them or shaming a child for feeling afraid of something does not teach a child anything useful. It also makes them feel less secure with the adults around them and therefore impacts on their brain development.

What adults must definitely never do is add to children's natural fears. Because children are young, vulnerable and inexperienced in life, they are afraid a lot. Any fears caused directly by the very people to whom the child looks for safety and protection are unbearable and are likely to cause a child to grow up with a traumatised brain.

Fear of Death

The biggest enemy of the limbic brain is death. Each individual in our species has evolved to have a profound fear of dying. We know that fear of death was effective at keeping our ancestors alive because we are still here and fear of death is still very much with us.

If each individual in a species that lives in a dangerous environment, is sufficiently afraid of death, it increases the survival rate of the entire species. Imagine a species where 85% of the individuals do not care much if they live or die. Such a species would be less likely to survive in an environment filled with dangers. Fear of death was useful for our survival in the conditions our species lived in. We are the descendants of those who survived long enough *because* they feared enough for their lives. Their genes were passed on to us and so we are all still driven by a powerful survival instinct and a natural fear of dying. This ancient fear of dying often hides behind our modern anxieties and fears, no matter how we try to rationalise them and what 'fancy' language or theories we use to describe them.

From this fear-based, survival-of-the-species perspective, individuals do not matter so much as individuals or unique beings. Our individuality, our unique identity, our need to express and develop our identity has little value to the collective. We each matter only in the role we play for the survival of our species.

Fear of death is central to how we organise ourselves into groups and societies. The more frightened a group or a society is, the more oppressive and controlling it is likely to be and the more conformity it will demand from its individual members. Oppression is not an expression of strength but of great fear and all oppressive regimes are, by necessity, driven by fear. The more fearful a society is the more control it tries to exercise over its individual members. From the point of view of the survival-of-the species, a 'good' or 'worthy' individual is someone who is most fearful of dying and who therefore obeys the rules the group decides are necessary for survival. Obedience is expected even it places individuals in conflict with themselves and their belief system. In fearful, oppressive societies, developing into a unique individual and seeking fulfilment of one's potential is only permitted provided it is not seen to contradict the group's primary drive to survive.

Safe/Unsafe

You can think of our limbic brain as existing in two states, *safe* or *unsafe*. When we feel safe, we are able to do all kinds of things that are not necessary for our immediate survival but are useful for long-term survival and development. We play, have fun, bond with others, groom ourselves and others, we collect food, look after our cave/house, learn, invent something new, feel interested. We feel motivated to get involved in things that happen around us, do something artistic or something for the fun of doing it. When we are safe we can also feel curious and motivated to explore and discover new things (provided they feel safe enough and do not trigger us into feeling under threat).

When we are not safe, everything, except for immediate survival, is temporarily pushed to the background and is placed on hold. The moment we feel unsafe, all other activities stop and we go into 'fight-flight-freeze' to make sure we survive and protect those who depend on us for their survival.

Most people's limbic brains work exactly as intended. When people feel 'frozen', 'stuck in a rut', when they suffer from 'writers' block' or feel apathetic and uninterested in what is going on around them, there is a good chance they feel under threat.

People often criticise themselves and others, including children and young people, for not being able to concentrate, for 'procrastinating' or for having a short attention span. Children cannot concentrate on their studies and cannot feel interested or engaged in learning when they are frightened and the truth is that none of us can. There is always a good reason if a person feels under threat, even if the threat is not obvious to others. As a therapist I always take people's fears seriously.

- If you are reading this right now, I am assuming you feel safe enough to concentrate on reading. Please pause for a moment. Look around you. Breathe. How do you feel? Can you see, hear or smell anything that makes you feel uneasy?

- If you do, you might find that your concentration and interest begin to fade and your attention will be drawn to the thing that might present a threat to you. If, hopefully, you notice nothing special, everything smells, looks, feels and sounds normal, you would be able to continue to concentrate on reading.

- Do you remember the last time you had trouble concentrating? Perhaps you found yourself reading the same paragraph over and over again? What was it that made it difficult for you to concentrate?

  Try to reflect on the threat you felt at the time. It could have been something wired from your past or something that troubled or worried you at the time. Either way, it would have affected your level of interest in what you were reading and your ability to concentrate and take it in.

Feelings / Emotions[9]

"And you would accept the seasons of your heart, even as you have always accepted the seasons that pass over your fields. And you would watch with serenity through the winters of your grief."– Khalil Gibran. *The Prophet.*

At the start of therapy almost every client wants to know if their feelings are 'normal'. New clients say things like, '*I feel x, y or z, but I shouldn't feel like this*', '*There is no reason for how I'm feeling*', or '*I do not like how I'm feeling, and I do not want to feel like this.*'

I remember having the same worries at the start of my own journey in therapy. It was understandable given my abusive history and the trauma it inflicted on me. (Trauma can make people feel deeply disturbing, intense feelings a lot more of the time than people who do not have trauma). When I saw my first therapist, I told him that all I wanted from him was to tell me if I was crazy… My feelings were so complex and hard to bear, I thought I was nuts. Whatever concerns people bring to therapy, they are always about suffering, and human suffering is always about feelings. Suffering is itself an emotional experience.

If everyone could do what Khalil Gibran advises in the above quote, therapists would not have a job. But most people have no idea about the 'seasons of their heart' – their feelings – what they are, and how to handle them.

It is no wonder people worry about their feelings when our society is so poorly informed, and so unskilled in handling feelings. In a misguided attempt to help, [10] I believe the medical and psychiatric professions have made things worse. The medicalisation[11] of mental

---

[9] I use the world 'feeling' and 'emotion' to express the same thing.

[10] I was told years ago that medicalising mental health was supposed to be helpful, because it removed the shame or stigma out of mental health. The idea was that if you see mental health difficulties as a medical problem, the person would not consider it their fault… Even if this were true, using bad science, or giving people the wrong information about what is going on with them only creates much bigger problems. For example, the 'chemical imbalance' hypothesis behind depression has been discounted already, and yet, one of the biggest interventions for depression (the diagnosis is often wrong, by the way) is medication.

[11] Medicalisation occurs when a medical framework is applied to non-medical issues, such as human psychological suffering. It then dictates how these problems are seen, managed or treated. If you are interested in reading a scholarly paper on the topic, have a look at Peter Conrad's

health has backfired, and is largely responsible for the mental health disaster we are facing.

People who feel bad, and are worried about how they feel, are told that their uncomfortable feelings are 'mental health problems', even an 'illness'. Any feeling other than contentment or happiness is classified as 'sick, which implies that only a happy or content human is a healthy human.

At this time in human history, most people are not so likely to meet a sabre-toothed tiger in the street outside their home, or on their way to work. Most of the dangers our limbic brain is primed to recognise no longer exist. It is therefore understandable that people worry that their fears and anxieties do not make any sense. But they always do.

We would not worry so much about our feelings if we are regularly reassured that what we feel is normal, especially during our childhood and youth. We would have a different relationship with our feelings if early in our life caregivers were *attuned* to our feelings accurately, and made us feel 'felt' (as Dan Siegel calls it). If adults helped us develop an 'emotional vocabulary' – the language to name and express our feelings and inner experience – we would be different than we are now.

Feelings have had a bad reputation as unreliable, volatile, or weak, and the opposite of common sense and reason. For millennia, and in some places even now, women were seen as more 'emotional'. This was an excuse to think of women as fickle, unreliable, child-like, and less intelligent than men, and to treat us as inferior. Males were considered less emotional, more rational, and therefore more reliable, and intelligent. This is all harmful nonsense. But it says a lot about our attitude to emotions.

Non-human mammals[12] feel what they feel. When they are happy, they are happy, when they are sad, they are sad. They do not try to understand their feelings, and they do not worry about them. They just *are*.

We are self-aware beings. When we feel something, we *know* we feel it. When we suffer, we *know* it. Self-awareness is probably *the* definitive characteristic of being human. It has the potential to make our life rich,

---

(Brandeis University) 1992 paper, 'Medicalization and Social Control' in the journal, *Annual review of Sociology*. 18:209-232. This paper offers an extensive review of the literature on the topic.

[12] I used to think that only mammals felt. But I have seen more recent research that suggests that insects might also have feelings.

and meaningful. It also makes us safer for one another, because it makes us see what we are doing. Without self-awareness we would not be able to regulate our behaviour (see the chapter below on the prefrontal cortex). The specific goal of Gestalt therapy, for example, is to help people increase their self-awareness, because it is essential for change. Until you know you are doing something, you cannot change it. But without the right support and guidance at the start of life, and throughout, our self-awareness can make life difficult. The way I see it, most people tend to suffer twice because they are self-aware. They feel uncomfortable feelings, *and* they worry about them.

What are feelings?

People would not spend so much energy worrying about theirs, or other people's feelings if they understood what they are. Our limbic brain's job is to keep each of us alive another day by helping us identify threats and survive them. Working together with our reptilian brain, our limbic system uses our five senses to scan our body, and our environment continuously. We listen for possible threats, watch, smell, taste, or identify potential threats through the sense of touch.[13] Much of this is automatic, and happens without awareness.

The limbic brain does not have language. Language is a highly advanced function made possible by our neo-cortex, our 'new' brain. Feelings are the ancient limbic brain's 'language', the way it tries to tell us if we are safe or unsafe. They are not strange, mysterious, or abnormal, and neither are they a sign of immaturity, or a 'malfunction'. The limbic brain's job is to react to the environment. Whatever is around us, is reflected back in the feelings that the limbic brain generates. Feelings are simply *information* about whether we are safe, or unsafe in any given moment. If the environment is dangerous, the limbic brain will react with feelings that reflect the threat, which then leads to the activation of our survival system.

Most people's limbic brains work exactly as they are supposed to work. This means that emotions are always there for a reason. Emotions provide a substantial proportion of the information that we need in

---

[13] The limbic brain does this even when we sleep. If you look at a sleeping cat, you'll notice that the cat's ears constantly move and are attuned to the environment. The cat would wake up instantly if she suddenly heard something unexpected. Our senses do the same.

order to be well, make good decisions, survive, and thrive. To ignore feelings is irrational.

Think of the limbic brain like the radar that you see in every airport, the one that turns constantly. The radar's role is to scan the airspace around the airport, and alert us to anything that might be up there, a flock of birds, a storm, or anything that could pose a threat to aircraft. The radar uses radio waves to scan the airspace. When the radio waves hit something solid, they bounce back. This translates into visual signals on the radar screen in the air traffic control tower. The air traffic controller understands what the signals on the screen could mean, and uses the information they provide to make good decisions to keep planes safe.

Our safety in the air depends on the correct interpretation of the signals on the radar screen, and on the decisions made by air traffic controllers. We trust that these skilled people pay attention to *all* the information, *all* the signals they see on their screens, and that they know what action to take in different situations. We cannot afford for air traffic controllers to ignore signals they do not 'like', or do not 'feel like' attending to.

Imagine if an air traffic controller looked at one of those blips on the radar screen and thought, *'I really do not like this blip, so I'm just going to ignore it'*, or *'I'm scared of this blip, so I'll turn away from it, and pretend it is not there'*. What if air traffic controllers did not have the skill to interpret the signals correctly and make good decisions, or if they were drunk on the job? This is how we are with our emotions. There is no wonder we suffer from so many 'crashes' inside, and that so many people experience their inner life as messy and unsafe.

> Emotions or feelings are the way our limbic brain communicates, or tries to communicate information that it considers essential to our survival.

The most important lessons about our emotions come from our childhood environment. Whatever children experience repeatedly is wired into their brain. The way adults handle children's feelings will become the default in children's brains. Children can learn to ignore, suppress, criticise, or medicate their feelings. They can learn to be afraid of them, fight them, worry that they are bad, wrong, or sick, or they might just act on them without any filters. I do not need to know too much about a client's childhood environment to get a good idea about what it was like. The way people react to, and handle their feelings at the start of therapy, reveals a great deal about what their childhood environment wired into their brain.

What the environment wires into our brain can either help us develop, or get in the way of our development. It is the latter that tends to bring people to therapy. I do not blame parents for this, especially parents from previous generations. Parents cannot teach what they do not know. We do have the knowledge now, and it is never too late to learn. It is especially important for our relationships, and for people who interact with children and young people.

Are feelings primitive, or a part of a primitive system? Probably, considering that our limbic brain is so ancient. If humanity continued to evolve, would we lose our capacity to feel in another hundred million years? No one knows, and frankly, I hope not. Our feelings have a way of offering 'colour' and 'texture' to our life, and to what we experience. They help us bond with others and our environment. While we do feel uncomfortable when we experience threat, our feelings also enable us to experience pleasure, wonder, enjoyment, warmth, attachment, and joy. I would never want to lose my capacity to feel.

There is no such thing as 'negative' or 'positive' emotions

Every time I hear or read the phrase 'negative emotions', I cringe. The idea that there are 'negative' or 'positive' emotions is out of touch with reality, and unscientific. Incorrect ideas about feelings lead to unhelpful, even harmful psychological practices. No matter how uncomfortable some emotions are, they are *not* a problem to be solved, dissected, or analysed. Neither are they something to fight, avoid, fix, change, medicate, or eliminate.

Most people's emotions are *consistent* with real life events and experiences. It could be past or present experiences, or both. Most people are sane. Therefore, emotions always make perfect sense if you know something about people's past and present circumstances. Treating emotions separately from the rich and complex context of a person's history, or present reality is harmful. It can reinforce the belief that their emotions are 'sick' or 'wrong', and it can make people feel even more 'crazy', 'sick', 'damaged', 'weak', or 'strange' than they already do.

If a friend betrayed you and it was a devastating experience at the time, it would be natural and functional to be cautious about new friendships, because your limbic brain has wired in the lesson that when you are close to someone you can get hurt. It will tell you that if you open your heart to someone new, what happened before, will happen again. While this may be limiting, the fear itself is completely normal given the circumstances. The important point is to remember that given the circumstances, the fear of being vulnerable and suffering another betrayal is not a malfunction. Our limbic brain is simply doing its job.

It looks like our society wants us to get rid of our 'bad' feelings, and a lot of people think this is what therapy is for. A new client once asked me half-jokingly if I could 'amputate' that part of him that feels so awful. I felt empathy, and understood why he said this. But trying to get rid of uncomfortable feelings is like trying to convince our body to never pee again. It damages us.

There are no shortcuts to enlightenment, maturity, or psychological wellbeing. Because of what our brain is, we cannot bypass or ignore feelings, no matter how uncomfortable they are. In fact, the more uncomfortable our feelings are, the more attention we need to pay to them. Either way, having uncomfortable feelings does not mean we are 'sick'.

Instead of the unhelpful idea of 'positive' or 'negative', it makes more sense to think of feelings as comfortable or uncomfortable. When our limbic brain assumes we are safe, we feel comfortable feelings (e.g., calmness, happiness, warmth, closeness, joy, enjoyment, hope, excitement, inspiration, motivation, etc.) Uncomfortable feelings (e.g., anger, fear, hatred, envy, insecurity, pain, etc.) are the limbic brain's way of communicating that it thinks we are unsafe.

No one comes to therapy because of their comfortable feelings. People worry only about the feelings that are uncomfortable, and this makes a great deal of sense. There is a logical, survival-based, evolutionary reason why we focus on our uncomfortable emotions. Uncomfortable emotions alert us that we might be unsafe. If we paid the same level of attention to fear, as we do to (comfortable) emotions like enjoyment, or calmness, we might not be careful enough when a threat is close. In other words, if we want to survive in an unpredictable and hostile environment filled with predators, it makes sense to focus on feelings that alert us to threats. Humanity survived and is growing in numbers despite extraordinary odds against us, *because* our limbic brain has been so fine-tuned and attentive to danger.

Real therapy needs to offer an opportunity to find out what our uncomfortable feelings are trying to tell us. What risks, or threats does our limbic brain perceive in our present circumstances, in our past, or both? If we consider uncomfortable feelings to be the problem to eliminate, all we are doing is trying to 'kill the messenger'. If we do not listen to our feelings, we cannot change what needs changing in our present situation, nor can we recover from a harmful past.

The point is that feelings are an accurate reflection of our environment. As I tell my clients, their feelings are not a malfunction. It is their environment, (past present, or both), that malfunctioned. For example, when a child grows up in an abusive family, it is the environment that is sick, not the child's feelings about it. In domestic abuse/coercive control, it is the abuser, and the environment they create, that is the problem, not how the victim feels about it.

The reason I know this with absolute certainty is because it is well-known... For example, well-established[14] studies on depression from decades ago, showed that depression is what happens when a mammal is in a bad situation, but does not have the power to change its circumstances. The mammal is in effect trapped and has no power to free itself. In other words, we know that the internal experience of depression is an accurate representation of the mammal's external circumstances. Like everything else that the limbic brain reflects from

---

[14] I do not want to describe the details of those studies, because they involve the unacceptable torture and abuse of sentient mammals. We did not need to abuse those poor defenceless animals to find out about depression. We could just speak to people to find out everything we need to know. If you really want to read about these studies on depression, you will find the details in most first year psychology textbooks.

the environment, depression simply mirrors precisely what goes on in people's lives (present, past, or both).

If someone is depressed, we need to find out what circumstances in their life are harmful to them, and are causing them pain. We also need to find out what (or who) is causing them to feel powerless to change their circumstances. As soon as people, or any mammal, are offered even a little bit of power to affect their circumstances, depression would disappear. If you have ever felt depressed and no one explained this to you, you have received incorrect, unscientific advice.

From the moment we are born our limbic brain wires in a 'catalogue' of dangers and risks, things we should be worried about. Our brain's perception of reality and what might be safe or unsafe for us depends on what we experienced or witnessed in childhood, and throughout life. We also learn about threats and dangers from witnessing other people's experiences, and from powerful stories, and cultural narratives.[15] The more powerful or dramatic the story, the more danger, fear, or suffering it contains, the more strongly and quickly our limbic system would wire it in.

When our limbic brain is in charge, our pre-wired catalogue of fears and experiences would determine how we interpret our reality. We compare everything new with our pre-wired catalogue. If the new situation does not quite fit, we would err on the side of caution, and try to make it fit. This is why there are so many misunderstandings between people in relationships.

From a limbic point of view, we are often at the mercy of interpreting the present from the point of view of what was wired in our past. What people believe they see or hear in a given moment, may not be what is really there. But if it looks, feels, sounds, even smells familiar, the limbic brain will make us feel the same feelings we felt when the original experience was wired in. A great deal of relationship therapy is about helping people see what is really in front of them, and not what their brain is wired to see.

Repetition wires our brain. If something was repeated enough times in our environment, it would become especially 'hardwired'. This

---

[15] From the moment we are born our limbic brain begins to wire a catalogue of all the things we should be scared of or worry about. Children look to their environment to learn how to respond to different situations. It is up to adults to help children understand what is really worth worrying about and what is not.

wiring contains a lot of what we think of as our character, our responses to situations, our preferences, likes or dislikes, our behaviours, our beliefs, and our emotional reactions in different situations.

If a child is repeatedly criticised, that experience would be wired in, along with every feeling the child felt each time they were criticised. Repetition reinforces the connections and creates a permanent neural network that contains the entire experience of criticism. This child would grow into an adult who is likely to be self-critical, who would expect criticism from others, might fear it, resent it, be crushed by it, etc. They might see criticism even if it is not there, because the other person's facial expression, body language, or tone of voice resemble those of the adult who criticised them in their past. If clients justify themselves a lot, I know that this is something they had to do as children. There is a good chance they were criticised often, doubted, or were repeatedly on the receiving end of mistrust.

If each time a child tries to communicate that they feel scared, they are told impatiently to just 'get on with it', this is what will be hard-wired into their developing brain. The child will grow into an adult who will be afraid of feeling fear, view it as a weakness, or feel impatient with themselves. They are likely to tell themselves to 'get on with it', and will believe that fear is dangerous, shameful, wrong, bad, or unacceptable to others.

This person did not consciously choose to believe any of this. In childhood their brain did exactly what it was supposed to do. It made them adapt to their environment in the best way possible, to maximise their chances of survival. Children's brains wire in accurately the requirements of their environment, what their caregivers approve or disapprove of, what they value, what they like or dislike, etc. Nature tries to make sure our caregivers want us, like us, and approve of us to increase the chances they would keep us alive, and help us develop. We do not choose our childhood environment, and have no control over what it wires into our brain.

We do not all respond emotionally the same way when faced with the same situation. That is because each of us carries unique sensitivities, which our past experiences wired into our brain. Each person's limbic system will report different information (emotions) depending on the person's unique history and experiences.

When the emotions we feel in a situation are different to other people's emotions, it does not mean that we (or they) are wrong, bad, crazy, unreasonable, sick, stubborn, or stupid. Our limbic brain offers each of us unique information (feelings) that is consistent with the environment that has shaped us and wired itself into us. This is one of the main reasons people must not judge other people's feelings. We genuinely do not know what it is like to 'walk in someone else's shoes', because we do not have their brain...

A few key points about emotions

• There is no such thing as 'good' or 'bad', 'right' or 'wrong' feelings. *All* emotions are *information,* and they are all equally valid.

• In most people the limbic brain works exactly as it is meant to, and does exactly what it has been wired to do.

• An uncomfortable emotion means that our limbic brain has a good reason to believe we are under threat. It is an alert, a signal that we are not safe.

• *All our emotions must be taken seriously,* regardless of whether there is a real threat in the present (a predator, violence, bullying, control, abuse, or something else), or whether it is an old threat wired into our limbic brain from our past that is triggered by something in the present. Either way, feelings are information that we need to listen to.

Feelings and behaviour

While the limbic system gives us our emotions, or in other words, information about what is going on, the *choice* about how to behave in response to those feelings should not be left for the limbic brain. In a world without sabre tooth tigers and giant hyenas, our choices and decisions should ideally come from our executive brain.

The limbic system has evolved for short-term, moment-to-moment survival. It is a reactive brain. It does not have the ability to 'think' rationally, plan for the future, or take a lot of information into consideration. In fact, when we are under threat, we would find it difficult to take in a lot of information, or think clearly. (This is a key point that I discuss later in the book). As adults, when faced with a threat, our limbic brain has a narrow range of options focused entirely on short-term survival. Our limbic options on how to respond to a threatening situation are variations on the instinctive fight-flight-freeze responses to threat. They are based on the unique way we fought, fled or froze in order to cope with our childhood environment.

When adults react out of their limbic brain in response to a difficult emotion, their behaviour might be problematic. We can understand if children make bad decisions about how to behave. They are reactive, they do not have a lot of life experience, they cannot regulate their emotions well, and they cannot see the 'bigger picture'. But we expect adults to behave differently. Adult behaviour carries much more weight, and responsibility, and has a much bigger impact than children's behaviour.

If we live with a parent who had a frightening tantrum each time they felt annoyed, or disappointed, we might grow up to be wary of annoyance or disappointment in ourselves or others. There is a risk we might identify these feelings with the behaviour we witnessed in our childhood. We might learn, for example, that anger leads to aggression, raised voices, abuse, or violence, that impatience or frustration lead to tantrums, pain ends up in drunkenness, and sadness or grief lead to collapse and dysfunction. It all depends on what we witnessed when we were young.

Children rarely follow only what they are told. We learn best by imitation, by watching what others *do*. Children can develop a negative impression of some feelings, because they witness the adults around them mishandle theirs. So, if an angry parent behaves violently, children can grow up into adults who avoid their own anger. This is because they associate anger with violence. Many clients have told me over the years, 'I do not *do* anger, I am not an angry person. When my father was angry he used to punch the walls and yell at us. I do not want to be like him'… Alternatively, a child can grow up into an adult who also lashes out violently verbally or physically when they are angry. This is how anger was expressed in the family, and this is what the child experienced as normal.

Another reason we might confuse emotions with behaviour is because there was no gap between them. If adults could not stop and think before they acted, if they just reacted to whatever they were feeling, we experienced their feelings and behaviour as if they were happening simultaneously.

We might confuse feelings with behaviour also because that is what we were taught to do. Children's feelings are often treated not like feelings, but like *problem behaviours*. When children *feel* something that adults do not like, or that makes adults feel uncomfortable, they can make them believe that just by *feeling* something they are *doing* harm to someone else. Children who grow up like this can turn into adults who believe that when they feel something, they are hurting other people. For example, if a feeling of anger was not allowed in the family, children can grow up to believe that feeling angry is wrong, regardless of how they act when they are angry.

It is important to remember that feelings are not the same as actions or behaviour. Behaviour or actions come after emotions. We cannot choose our feelings, but well-developed adults have the capacity to choose their behaviour. As we grow and develop, we are better able to think before we act. No matter what we feel, we can take our time to decide how to behave. The more developed we are, the bigger the time gap between our feeling and our behaviour.

Children do not always know how to express what they feel or need. They are more likely to act it out in their behaviour. Adults need to be careful not to focus on the behaviour, but see it for what it is, a form of communication. They need to separate children's emotions, what the child experiences inside, from what the child is doing, and try to attune to what the child's behaviour is trying to communicate. If adults focus only on the child's behaviour, the child will grow up to believe that feelings, and behaviour are the same.

About the dynamics of emotions/feelings

Any emotion we try to block in ourselves or in others will try to 'push' through anyway. From our limbic system's point of view, our lives might depend on communicating the emotion successfully. The feeling, the information will not just go away, it will try to complete its cycle because in times of threat, survival is the limbic brain's top priority.

This is especially true for strong emotions. Strong feelings can be triggered in response to a perceived threat in the present, or by 'unfinished business' from the past. If feelings are *overwhelming*, they are likely to be 90% in the past, and only 10% in the present. Feelings that are just about the present and have no links to anything in the past, will not feel particularly intense. They will also fade away quickly, and will not be much of a problem.

> ## A Useful Rule of Thumb
> If feelings are overwhelming, they are
> probably
> 90% in the past, and only 10% in the
> present.

A trigger is what happens when (from a limbic point of view) there is some similarity between something that is happening now, and something threatening from the past. Even if it is only a trigger to the past, and there is no threat now, the limbic brain cannot help but communicate its message. If the message does not get through, the limbic system will continue to think that we are at risk, and will not stop until we pay attention.

There are many examples of unacknowledged or blocked emotions trying to push through to complete their natural cycle. Blocked or ignored grief, sadness, or helplessness can develop into depression. Anger can transform into rage, pain in the neck, upper arms, upper back, or shoulders, or into a headache.

The diagram on the next page shows the dynamic of emotions. Remember that emotions are information about our environment that tells us if we are safe or unsafe in any given situation. A trigger, something in our environment, would cause an emotion to start (anything can be a trigger, and triggers are unique to each person). The emotion would then escalate and reach a peak. If it is heard properly and validated, it would complete its natural cycle and will not persist.

If the emotion is allowed to complete its cycle, it would often lead to an insight. Insight is that 'aha' moment when we understand the reason we felt the way we did in a situation. Knowing ourselves depends a great deal on the way we relate to our emotions. The more we validate our emotions and allow them to flow and complete their cycle, the more we learn about ourselves. It is also the key to change and development as you will see later in this book.

If we block the emotion, the cycle cannot complete itself and the information is not transmitted, or received successfully. Most people come to therapy with a huge backlog of 'blocked' emotions. Blocks can be caused by messages that people give to themselves or others. The list below the graph offers a few examples. Can you identify anything familiar in that list? What would you add to it?

The circle at the bottom of the diagram tries to say that because the human mind seeks completion, emotions will not just go away. They will always try to complete their cycle somehow. Displaced anger is a good example of the brain's attempt to complete an emotional cycle.

If your boss made you angry, and you blocked it because you could not communicate it, or sort it out with them, you might end up taking your anger out on your partner and children at home. You might find something said, did, or did not do irritating. In the that moment, you would truly believe that they are causing your anger. But it is possible your brain is just trying to complete the cycle of emotion that you had to block at work. (If the emotion is overwhelming, you might need to consider that it was not even the boss that was the real source of your anger. It is possible that what happened with your boss triggered something from your distant past).

Emotions are often out of awareness. People might realise they were angry only *after* they have already blown up in the wrong place or time or at the wrong people (not that blowing up is ever the right, or moral thing to do).

The Dynamics of Emotions

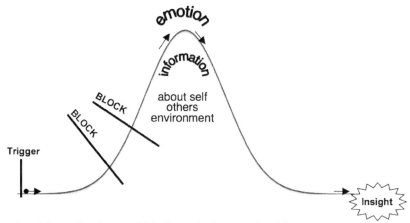

Examples of (internal and external) blocks to a healthy emotional flow:

- WHY do you / I feel like this?
- I don't have time for this. I have things to do.
- What's the point of feeling this?
- Boys don't cry!
- It's not nice for girls to be angry.
- I hate feeling angry / sad / hurt / disappointed
- You're upsetting your mother / father.
- I / you SHOULD be over this by now.
- I don't want to be seen as weak.
- What will people think of me?
- I SHOULD be happy.
- Others have bigger problems. I don't have a right to feel this.
- I'm scared that if I start crying I'll never stop.
- I MUST do / eat something to cheer myself up.
- I'm scared to feel like this.
- Feeling anything other than happy is wrong / sick, etc....

> **Assumption:**
>
> Emotional, behavioural or physical problems are symptoms of a lifetime of blocked emotional cycles.

Note: *If the normal emotional cycle is not allowed to be completed, it will try to complete itself somehow!*

Identify Your Blocks

• What feelings are you more likely to try to block in yourself and/or in others?

• Who taught you, or how do you think you learned to block those emotions?

• How do you block them? What do you tell yourself or others, or what do you do to stop yours or someone else's emotions?

• What do you think/worry might happen if you *did not* block those emotions, and allowed them to complete their natural cycle?

Mishandling Children's Feelings

Children's feelings are no less intense than those of adults. In fact, babies, toddlers, and children are likely to feel even more strongly than adults do. Children operate almost exclusively from their mammal (limbic) brain, and live in a fear-based, predominantly feeling world. Their developing executive functions do not become accessible until much later, around age fifteen. Among other things, it means that they cannot regulate their emotions, and need their caregivers to do it for them.

Children are also vulnerable for much longer than the young of other species. They look to adults for protection, safety, and guidance right into early adulthood. Children do not have enough life experience. They rely on adults to teach them what is worth worrying about, and what is not. For example, if a child receives the same extreme reaction to dropping a glass of juice on the floor, that they do to running into the road in front of traffic, they would not learn that one incident is much more serious than the other. To the child, breaking a glass by accident would feel as dangerous as being careless on the road.

If children's emotions are not handled correctly, children will carry their childhood fears and anxieties into adulthood, often without the language to express them, or the ability to make sense of them. Children need to be taught what their feelings mean, and be reassured that they are consistent with what is happening around them.

Children always try to communicate what they feel because they need to survive, and because their survival depends on the adults around them. They will do anything to try and get their message across.

As I discussed earlier, if a child acts out and displays annoying or disruptive behaviour, it is most likely because they are not able to communicate their feelings successfully to significant adults. Children's repeated experience might have already taught them that their feelings are likely to be mishandled. Children will stop trying to share how they feel if they learn that it is pointless, or that sharing how they feel exposes them to potential abuse or harm.

Children are not in a position to say to adults, '*You need to validate how I feel, because this is what my limbic brain needs in order to feel that you have heard my problem and that you'll keep me safe*'. Children do not have that kind of awareness yet, so they will try to express what they need the best way they know how.

Anxiety in adulthood is a direct result of mishandled emotions in childhood. Even people who grew up in non-abusive, otherwise loving families often grow into anxious adults. That is because even loving, and safe parents do not always handle their children's emotions correctly.

Mishandling children's (or anyone's) feelings can take the form of trying to **distract, interrogate** or **demand that they explain 'why'** they feel the way they do, **making fun** of the feelings, **mocking** or **shaming**, **dismissing** them, **belittling** or **minimising**, **comparing** the person's feelings to someone else's, **trying to control** or **criticising** the feeling, **accusing**, **using emotional pressure, threatening**, **rationalising** the feelings away, **ignoring**, **rejecting** the feelings, **brutalising** the person or **pathologising**, and **teasing**.

The table below lists examples of how children's feelings are mishandled. Most of the examples come from what clients have told me about the way adults responded to their feelings in their childhood. Some examples come from my experience, and also from what I witness when I see interactions between adults and children. I have left space at the bottom of the table for you to add more categories and examples from your own experience and observations.

You will notice that I have bunched together 'shaming' with the 'making fun, mocking, and humiliating' category. But I believe that *all* the ways that children's feelings are mishandled are in fact shaming. Shaming is always about control, and control is harmful at any age, because it interferes with healthy growth and development.

One of the reasons people treat children's emotions poorly, is because, for whatever reason, those feelings trigger something in them. In fact, when children's emotions trigger their caregivers, it is a sign that the adults might have unfinished business to attend to, and integrate once and for all. Either way, it is something for adults to look into, not for children to bear.

Notice how in some of the examples, feelings are confused with behaviour. When the child feels something that others do not like, they treat it as if the child is *doing* something wrong. All adults who deal with children need to pay attention here. I hear plenty of stories of teachers for example, mishandling children's feelings. The brutality of this is far less these days than it used to be. But even subtle mishandling of feelings is harmful to human development.

The severity of mishandling varies. There are families that mishandle feelings, but there is no abuse. In loving and safe families parents are usually open to feedback, and are more than willing to reflect on what they do, and learn to respond better to their children's feelings.

In abusive families, parents are not willing, or are unable to learn new and better ways to relate to their children. They are likely to get defensive, and argue that they know how to raise their children, and do not need parenting advice. A common excuse for mishandling children's feelings is that children 'should not be mollycoddled', and need to be 'toughened up'. Some parents say that this is what they experienced in their own childhood, and that 'it did them no harm'... They are obviously blind to the irony of it.

This table is included in my book on anxiety, in a chapter on the childhood origins of anxiety. But the examples in the table are not limited to children. Adults mishandle each other's feelings all the time in many contexts, including therapy. As a society we pay a heavy price for this because it makes everyone feel unsafe, and no one does well or grows when they feel unsafe. To help one another grow and be well, we need to respond to feelings correctly. The importance of responding correctly to our own, and other people's feelings is a central point in this book, which I cover it in some detail later.

Examples of incorrect responses to emotions	
Distracting	• "Come on, let's play with your new toy lorry" • "Let's have your favourite ice cream. That will make you feel better." • "Go do something useful. You'll feel better."
Interrogating	• "*Why* are you feeling like this?" • "I won't help you if you don't tell me why you feel like this."
Making fun of the child for feeling something / mocking / shaming / humiliating	• "Oh, look at her, she is a sour puss again…" • "Here start the waterworks again..." • "Always with the drama"… • "Oh, God, here we go again" … • "What are you a girl? You're such a wuss? • "Crying makes you weak"

Dismissing	<ul><li>"Do not be silly, of course your friends like you"</li><li>"Do you have any idea what it was like for me when I was your age? I had something to be sad about, but you have everything. You don't have any reason to be upset."</li><li>"Are you upset again? I really do not have time for your drama and moods!"</li><li>"It's all in your head."</li></ul>
Demonstrating impatience / lack of interest	<ul><li>"I do not have time for one of your moods now. You know how busy I am…"</li></ul>
Belittling, minimising	<ul><li>"Are you still upset about this? Don't be silly, it's nothing."</li><li>"You always make such a big deal of things…"</li><li>"Silly billy"</li><li>"Children are starving in the world. You think you have problems?"</li></ul>
Comparing	<ul><li>"Your sister doesn't react like this! Why cannot you be more like her?"</li><li>"Only stupid people feel like this."</li><li>"I was much braver than you at your age"</li></ul>
Controlling	<ul><li>"What are you so happy about? We both know it will end up in tears."</li><li>"We all know what is going to happen now"…</li><li>"In this family I am the only one who is allowed to be angry."</li><li>"You know we don't like a sad face in this family"…</li><li>"Stop this right now, and go do your homework!"</li></ul>

Criticising	• "Why do you always have to be upset?" • "What's wrong with you?" • "Are you stupid or something?" • "You shouldn't feel like this." • "You need to be braver than this"
Accusing	• "You must have done something to deserve it…"
Using emotional pressure	• "You know that I do not like to see you sad. It makes me upset." • "Look what you did. You made everyone upset now." • "Are you saying that I am not a good mother?" • "You are upsetting your father." • "You're ruining it for everyone."
Threatening	• "Don't you dare be angry with me, I am your mother/father". • "Just do as you are told, or else" … • "I'll give you something to cry about!" • "If you keep being like this, I'm going to send you away."
Rationalising	• "It doesn't make sense to feel upset about this. You need to think about this differently…" • "You're overreacting." • "What is the point of feeling like this? It won't change anything". • "You need to concentrate on the positives."
Ignoring	The adult caregiver is there, but is indifferent, does not engage with the child at all, walks out of the room, continues to do their activity, turns their face away from the child, or keeps their back turned, etc.

Rejecting	• "Go to your room, and come back when you can put a smile on your face." • "If you are going to cry, go somewhere else." • "I do not want to see you like this. Go wash your face and come back here." • "I wish I wasn't your father/mother" • "I didn't ask for this"
Punishing	The adult punishes the child for feeling something the adult doesn't like, for example, by giving the child the 'cold shoulder' and withdrawing. Other examples are locking the child away in their room, and depriving them of food, or other forms of violence. Punishing children for how they feel is a form of rejection and control.
*Brutalising / using violence **Violence against children is a crime, but it is still done behind closed doors.)**	• "This (slap, smack, or other brutal behaviour) will give you something to cry about." • Locking a child away in a room or worse.
Pathologising the feelings (making someone believe that their feelings are sick)	• "You're not well. We need to take you to the doctor" • "You need therapy" • "We need to get you pills. How you feel is not right"
Teasing	• "You'd be so much prettier if you had a smile on your face." • "No wonder no one likes you."

Feel free to add your own examples	

Adults' minds, or inner world, provide the blueprint for children's minds and inner reality. Or rather, the way adult brains are wired, provides the template for the way that children's brains will be wired, as well as what will be wired into them. It is as if the child's brain 'copies' the parent's brain. Parents cannot take their children further than their own psychological development. Therefore, children tend to leave home with a level of development that is similar to that of their parents. We cannot argue with this. It is just how humans are.

Children wire not just what is said directly to them but also what they witness and sense. The way parents or significant adults handle their own feelings is likely to become the basis for children's attitude to their own feelings. For example, a parent who is kind with her child's feelings, but not her own, sends a confusing message that there is one rule for the child, and a different rule for the parent. What children would learn is exactly that, that there is one rule for them, and another rule for other people. When these children grow up, they are likely to repeat what their parents did. They would be kind to others, but not to themselves.

No child wants to see their adult caregivers suffer. From the child's perspective, a suffering adult might not be able to be strong or fit enough to protect them. This can lead to children becoming 'parentified', that is spending their energy taking care of their parents' emotions to try to ease the parents' suffering. They do this in the hope that eventually their parents would be able to take care of them. Either way, it is a huge and unacceptable burden on children, and it interferes with their development. Parentified children could grow into over-responsible adults who try to 'fix' or rescue everyone. Alternatively, they might grow into adults who do not respect their parents, or anyone in position of authority, because they perceive adults as weak and unreliable.

Ideally adults who care for children should have a reasonably peaceful inner world. This doesn't mean not having 'issues'. It means not having too much internal conflict, not having bits of themselves fighting internally with other bits. Adults who are in a state of war with themselves are bound to suffer from anxiety. High levels of anxiety in adults can lead, not only to anxiety, but even to trauma symptoms in children[16]. Trauma is caused by a long-term inability to relax, and children do not feel secure around adults who are anxious, even if those adults are kind.

Even without any abuse, when children's feelings are handled clumsily or carelessly, they are likely to feel unloved, unseen, or misunderstood. The sad truth is that their instincts are correct. Parents who love their children, but regularly mishandle their feelings, are not *acting* lovingly. Children depend on love, and love is not just a warm and fuzzy feeling, caring for the physical needs of the child, or engaging with the child intellectually. Love is expressed in the most powerful way in how we respond to emotions.

Can you see how confusing it can be for children who are told regularly that they are loved, but whose feelings are also regularly mishandled? They are told they are loved, but when they come to the parent with a difficult emotion, they do not *feel* loved, because of the parent's unhelpful response.

Children would do anything for acceptance and approval. If feeling sad is not acceptable in the family, children would learn to push sadness away, and put a smile on their faces just to be accepted. Over time, this would cause certain experiences to go into a kind of 'quarantine' in the brain. There they would remain as an unintegrated clusters of neurons, which are the basis for our emotional triggers. These clusters of neurones are like 'time bombs', or 'landmines' that can 'explode' whenever the right button is pressed.

---

[16] You can read more about trauma and what causes it in my booklet, *Trauma and Its Impact: What you need to know.*

When so many emotional experiences are quarantined over many years of being mishandled in the same way, people can grow into adults who are 'out of touch' with their feelings, or inner reality.

Learning Good Emotional Skills

- Next time someone (a partner, colleague, friend, a child, a young adult, one of your students) tells you how they feel about something, notice what you say in response. What is your *habitual* response to other people's feelings?

- Do you feel an obligation to make the person 'feel better', or help them out of their emotion somehow?

- Do you consider an uncomfortable emotion a *problem* to be solved?

- Reflect on where you have learned to respond to other people's emotions the way you do. Was it done to you? Did/do you see others around you acting this way with each other?

- Next time someone tells you (or shows you) how they feel, try to validate their emotion. Validation means telling someone that it is OK to feel the way they do.

- Pay close attention to how it feels for you to do it. What do you notice about your own inner experience when you validate someone else's emotion? Is it comfortable, uncomfortable, does it feel silly or pointless, is it easy or difficult, do you feel helpful or unhelpful? Whatever you feel, validate your own emotion as well (more on this later in the book).

- What do you notice about the other person's reaction after you have validated their emotion?

The Neocortex & the Prefrontal Cortex (PFC)

Our third brain is called the neocortex, 'neo' from the Greek for 'new'. The neocortex is the newest and largest brain we have and in humans it is extremely complex. It sits on top of, and covers, the two older brains. Our neocortex allows us to perform functions that are uniquely human. It has changed our physical bodies and has made it possible for us to invent technology, perform complex tasks, develop language and writing and create the complex social and technological world we live in now and everything that it contains.

The part of our neocortex that is most significant to psychotherapy, and to our mental health and growth, is our *prefrontal cortex* (PFC), the 'executive brain'. It is located at the very front part of the neocortex. If you draw a vertical line from the middle of each of your eyebrows upwards, it can be found in the area between these two lines, on either side of the 'third eye' (the spot midway between your eyebrows).

The prefrontal cortex is the central processing unit of the entire brain. It processes and organises an amazing amount of information that comes from all over the body and nervous system and from our environment. It coordinates our most advanced functions. Recent studies show that the PFC regulates what we call 'consciousness', something we recognise and experience but cannot yet explain or understand. It is our PFC and the executive functions it gives us that make our species unique and makes us 'human' (as opposed to being 'just' a mammal). It is the part of us that gives us the sense of being adults who can manage complex tasks in a complex world, and who can take responsibility for our actions and behaviours, and the way we impact on others.

The PFC is something of a mystery. It is the latest part of the brain to develop in our species and also in each one of us. It begins to develop as soon as we are born but 'kicks in' (if all goes well) around the age of fifteen [17]. Some parents might recognise the moment their child suddenly becomes more conscious of others and more aware of themselves. It's as if suddenly someone turns on the light. It can happen in an instant. One minute they are still a child and the next minute they

---

[17] I have heard a few stories over the years of incredible young children who seem to have executive abilities like empathy and insight that appear far beyond their years. I suspect that in a small number of children the prefrontal cortex 'turns on' earlier than fifteen.

begin to demonstrate traits that we associate with being an adult. People often describe it as the moment when everything changed for them. It can be incredibly frightening to become self-aware, to suddenly see the things that are 'wrong' around you and become aware that you are suffering.

Many young people who are not brought up safely and lovingly, often begin to exhibit psychological and behavioural problems and 'act out' after their prefrontal cortex has kicked in. They had obviously suffered before, but now they *know* they feel uncomfortable and it can be overwhelming without the right support.

The prefrontal cortex is a highly specialised area of our modern brain. It can easily be damaged or compromised by drugs or alcohol. Its functions, as far as we know, cannot be replaced or taken over by any other part of the brain. Once the PFC is gone, it's gone. The prefrontal cortex is so important for human relationships and for our psychological wellbeing, that looking after it should be everyone's priority.

The prefrontal cortex gives us a long list of incredible, uniquely human abilities. All of these abilities are crucial for our functioning as mature adults and in relationship with others. They are called 'executive' or 'higher' functions. In other places you might see lists of nine functions of the executive brain but my list is much longer. It is based on my observations from my work and my own life experiences.

Our Executive Functions

Compassion – Compassion to everyone and everything including ourselves is easy from the PFC, and it comes naturally. It is unconditional and inclusive and is available in abundance.

There is no 'compassion fatigue' or burnout in the PFC. We can be compassionate and kind indefinitely, provided that we are careful to meet our own needs. But meeting our own needs is also natural for the PFC. It balances our own needs with the needs of others naturally and with ease.

When our limbic brain's needs are not met (when the limbic brain is in charge), we might feel that we have to force ourselves to act kindly or compassionately towards others and ourselves. It is normal to feel resentful and exhausted if we do this too much.

From the limbic brain we extend compassion conditionally and selectively. Limbic compassion is only possible if we are OK, if we are not under threat, and usually only when we feel good about someone.

Unconditional love – The prefrontal cortex gives us the capacity to experience mature, unconditional, indiscriminatory love that is not based on need. The kind of love we experience from our PFC is not tribal. It does not depend on what others give us, or do for us, whether or not they help us survive, who they are, or even if they love us back. Everyone matters and we seem to be able to love everything and everyone unconditionally.

Attunement - The prefrontal cortex enables us to be attuned to what someone else is going through. It is a kind of aware sensitivity to other people's inner experience. Dan Siegel[18] talks about the ability to make others 'feel felt'. The PFC is the part of the brain that enables us to communicate to others that we *see* them and their inner experience, and that we are *with* them. We can often do this with just a look. If you are on the receiving end of attunement, you just know. You *feel* that the other person *sees* you.

Empathy – Empathy from the prefrontal cortex is *different* to the limbic brain's ability to *resonate* with other people's inner states, or feel their feelings.[19] We can feel someone else's feelings, but if the PFC is not in charge, we might not care much about it. It might even feel like an annoying burden, or a threat. When children feel a parent's distress, they care about it because it is a threat to their own survival and well-being. Before the PFC starts to work, they do not think of their parents as separate people, and cannot experience real empathy for them. They have no choice because they are dependent on adults and cannot manage on their own.

Some people whose PFC does not work properly (e.g., people with a personality disorder) might know what others are feeling, but they

---

[18] See Daniel Siegel's book, *Mindsight*.
[19] See section on the 'mirror neurons' in my booklet on relationships

might enjoy their suffering or use their feelings against them. Anyone who has been on the receiving end of psychological abuse and manipulation would recognise this.

The PFC gives us the ability to come close to what it is like to be the other person in a particular moment, *and* care about it. It also gives us the instinctive insight into how best to be with the other person in that moment, to maintain not only their physical wellbeing, but their integrity and wholeness.

Self-awareness – Self-awareness is the ability to look inward into ourselves and 'see', or know what we are feeling, thinking, or doing. It is an insight into ourselves. (I discuss self-awareness in more detail in the section on emotions).

Planning and decision-making – The prefrontal cortex gives us the ability to take in a stupendous amount of information from a huge number of sources, analyse it, and make *long-term* plans and adult, rational decisions.

In this process of planning and decision-making, we consider not only what affects us directly or immediately. We consider the 'bigger picture', other people and circumstances, as well as the long-term consequences. It gives us the ability to be pro-active. Unlike the limbic brain, the PFC is not reactive and is not limited to past experiences and our pre-wired 'database' of past experiences and reactions.

Intuition – Everyone experiences intuition from time to time. Intuition is the ability to take in enormous amount of information we are not always conscious we are taking in. The PFC then processes and analyses this information extremely fast, and comes up with a solution, an answer, and insight, or an idea. Intuition works so fast, we do not recall collecting the information, tracking it, sorting through it, or analysing it. It can feel like a 'knowing' that comes out of nowhere.

The limbic brain, by contrast, relies on data from the five senses. It does not trust what it cannot see, hear, smell, touch, taste, remember, track, or grasp, and does not trust the unfamiliar. It can therefore make us doubt our intuition, ignore it, or go against its advice. To our limbic brain, an intuition that turns out to be correct can feel like 'magic', a miracle, something that is unlikely or impossible.

Perspective and objectivity – The prefrontal cortex gives us the ability to 'stand back' from a situation and look at it from a broader, more objective perspective. Because the limbic brain is so focused on our individual, moment to moment survival, it can be 'selfish', 'self-absorbed', and 'self- focused'. It gets emotionally entangled in many situations, especially when it believes we are under threat. Our limbic brain judges every situation according to how it affects *us*, or how well it serves our particular survival-based interests. Our PFC however, can look at how we fit in the 'bigger picture', and make us see and know that we are not the most important, or only person around. Perspective and objectivity are crucial for safe, peaceful, and growth-promoting relationships.

Emotional and behavioural regulation – The PFC is built to interact with our emotions and regulate them. Emotions are information that the prefrontal cortex needs in order to make good decisions. Our PFC can communicate to the limbic brain that it has successfully received its information, and that it will now take care of things. This helps the limbic brain settle down and relax. This is when our emotions feel well-regulated, and do not 'run away with us'.

The PFC is also able to regulate our behaviour. It can choose actions, responses, or any other behaviour that are not just habitual, 'kneejerk reactions', pre-wired by our past experience, or our species' evolution. If you feel intense anger, but your PFC is properly engaged, you will not 'lash out' at someone else. You will be able to feel your anger, at the same time as effortlessly knowing that you have a *choice* about how to behave.

If your anger offers information about something that is happening now, you will be able to address the present situation with clarity, wisdom, consideration for yours and others' welfare, and with perspective. If your anger provides information about the past, you will take the appropriate action to help yourself integrate that past, so it is no longer triggered and does not determine your present behaviour and responses. The limbic brain is reactive. Without the PFC to regulate it, it would tend to react, and act out whatever it feels for the purpose of short-term survival.

72

Fearlessness – The PFC does not seem to have the same fear-based herd instinct that our mammal brain has, and it does not seem to 'feel' fear. In fact, feelings are generated exclusively in the limbic brain. The PFC does not *feel* much at all, except for a kind of benevolent concern and compassion for everyone and everything, irrespective of whether they are members of our particular group or tribe.

If you look closely when people say they only have one or two options in a situation, you would almost always find that they are afraid. Some people might withdraw when they are scared, others might lash out, eat, smoke, shop, or drink. They might try to please or placate the person that triggers them, or otherwise comply, and choose the path of least resistance. It all depends on what was reinforced and hardwired into their limbic system in the past and throughout life.

The limbic system would tend to choose the option with the least amount of discomfort, because it perceives this as the safest. If people 'gang up' on someone at work, would you join the 'gang', or would you stick by that person and risk rejection from the rest of the group?

Our limbic brain would tell us to put ourselves first, but our PFC would tell us to do the right thing, and would not feel afraid to do it. Our PFC would guide us to act in ways that are not driven or motivated by fear.

Need for meaning and purpose – This is a particularly interesting and tricky function of our PFC. As mammals we do not need a reason, or justification to be alive. We are born, so here we are. Death is the enemy of our survivalist limbic brain, so we naturally want to live as long as possible, possibly for ever. We have no individual purpose other than ensuring we live long enough to make more copies of ourselves and pass on our genes, so that our species continues to exist.

Our PFC seems to have other ideas, or another 'agenda'. It cares less about *how long* we live, and much more about *how* we live. The PFC tells us that our existence needs to be *meaningful*. The PFC makes us *need* a purpose, and a reason for being. According to our PFC it seems that the survival of our species is not enough of a reason for humans to exist. Life has to mean something, and has to be for a purpose other than mere survival.

It can be a problem for mammals that 'merely existed' for many millions of years, to suddenly 'wake up' to a feeling that survival is not enough, and that life also has to mean something. Our PFC will not allow us to just exist from moment to moment like unaware mammals without paying a heavy price. It is usually our psychology or 'mental health' that suffers when people just survive and cope from day to day. It is an extraordinary and difficult contradiction to carry inside one head.

People who have a well-developed PFC (I believe it is most people), have a natural sense of 'mission' about their lives, and a sense of direction and purpose.[20] They have a feeling that they have some kind of a duty to use their lives for a purpose. As mammals, our purpose is given to us by nature, but the PFC gives us the option of *choosing* our purpose. Whatever we choose to do, and however we decide to use our life, our skills and talents, it has to be *meaningful* to us. What is meaningful to each of us seems to be linked with our values. If what we do contradicts our values, we can experience a deep conflict within ourselves.

You might have a well-paid job and enjoy the benefits it offers, and the experience of being 'successful' in our society's terms. It might offer you status, might boost your self-esteem, not to mention your bank balance. Perhaps what you do is important, and might even provide a a valuable service, and a benefit to others. But it might not carry much meaning for you personally, and it might not feel like *your* purpose. People who do menial jobs, or those working on production lines in factories, are not the only ones who can feel like generic, and replaceable cogs in big machines.

I meet many clients who have better paid jobs than factory workers, with better conditions, pay and status. If what they do does not align with their sense of purpose (beyond financial survival), they too would eventually have to face their PFC's demand for meaning and purpose.

Perhaps you have always worked hard, and have put your work ahead of your family. At some point, your PFC would make you realise what you are doing. At that point you might start to notice that your loved ones are suffering, and begin to see the impact your choices have on them. Your PFC tells you that relating to your children properly,

---

[20] To what degree we would be able to fulfil our 'mission', follow our sense of direction and fulfil our potential will depend on how integrated our limbic brain is with the functions of our PFC. (See chapter: Neural Integration).

and spending more time with them might be more important than your career.

Some people become aware of, and start to care about the harm their employer might be doing to people or the environment. They might feel that they want to do something that fits with their values, and that does no harm.

Whatever the situation, when people's need for purpose is not met, and they feel like they are wasting their precious time on Earth, it would lead to an 'existential crisis'. It is intensely uncomfortable, but it is a wakeup call, and it carries the potential for change and growth towards our unique potential. Many people come to therapy when they experience an existential crisis.

Purpose and meaning are unique to each individual. No one can tell anyone else what their purpose should be, or what would, or should give meaning to their particular life. Some parents who push their children into certain careers, usually think more about the child's economic survival and their status, rather than their fulfilment. I do not blame them. But raising young humans involves a great deal more than just helping them survive.

It seems that our sense of meaning and purpose is almost always tied up with making a positive contribution to others, to something 'bigger than ourselves'. Living a purposeful life filled with meaning makes us feel that we are living the 'right' life and it also benefits the world.

If, however, our limbic brain is mostly in charge of our life and our choices, it would override the PFC, and would make us choose survival over meaning and purpose. This usually results in psychological suffering, including anxiety.

Higher-level spirituality – The prefrontal cortex gives us the ability to have a spiritual life without being religious, and without having a particular deity to worship, a group to belong to, or rituals to perform. We do not need someone in authority to tell us what is right or wrong, how to think about ourselves, life or the universe, what to believe or what to do. We just know for ourselves.

Unlike the fear-based limbic system, our PFC has no need for certainty. Because it is not afraid of death, it is OK with the unknown. It is absolutely fine and at peace knowing that nothing is certain, that we cannot control anything, and that death is inevitable. It feels safe naturally, because it knows that we are not our bodies, but that there is a lot more to life and to us than we currently realise.

Whether or not there is something out there in the universe,[21] it seems to me that the 'antenna' to connect with it is in the prefrontal cortex. It is the PFC that gives us the ability to perceive something bigger than ourselves, and feel a connection to it.

Conscience, personal ethics and morality – Our prefrontal cortex gives us our conscience. It lets us *know* when we do something wrong and makes us *care* about it. We do not need parents, the police, the law, a priest, or anyone else to tell us when we do wrong. We know, and we care for the right reasons.

If we all operated from the prefrontal cortex most of the time, we would not need a criminal justice system to tell us that it is not OK to break into someone else's home and take their things. We would just know.

If our politicians, civil servants, or corporate leaders were able to operate from their PFC much more of the time, they would be able to take responsibility for their mistakes, rather than deflect, avoid, lie, become defensive, or look for scapegoats. They would be motivated by more than just self-interest, and would seek to make amends if they committed a crime, acted immorally, or carelessly. When you witness real courage, someone standing up for others or for what is right, even against a hostile mainstream, what you are seeing is the PFC in action.

The PFC gives us the ability to own up, take responsibility and make amends, sometimes at a great personal cost[22]. But it is OK because doing the right thing out of concern for others is its own virtue, and the PFC does not expect to be rewarded.

By contrast, the limbic brain might know that we did something wrong, but like everything else limbic, this too is motivated by fear and a narrow self-interest. Children are predominantly limbic. They can, and do feel guilty when they know that they have broken the rules. But

---

[21] I believe that consciousness is not produced by the complexity of our brain, but is everywhere and precedes matter. Some physicists call it, pan-psychism. If you are interested in learning more check out the Scientific & Medical Network (SMN), and its project, the Galileo Commission.

[22] If you haven't already seen it, I recommend the 2012 film 'Flight' with Denzel Washington. It perfectly demonstrates this point, especially towards the end. I'm afraid I cannot say any more without spoiling the film for you…

they will tend to worry more about getting caught, and about how getting caught would impact on *them*, rather than about what is moral or ethical.

The limbic brain can make us resent anyone who 'makes us feel guilty' when they point out that we had done something wrong. From a limbic point of view, we would rather not be confronted with the negative consequences of something we did. We simply cannot handle that kind of responsibility. If people operate from their limbic brain, they can lash out at the very people they hurt, because guilt makes them feel uncomfortable and they do not want to feel like this. This is why having the PFC in charge is so important to our maturity and ability to live with one another safely, morally and ethically.

Awareness of how we affect others & caring about it – Our prefrontal cortex makes us aware that we are each unique, *and* that we are not more valuable than anyone else. It gives us the ability to recognise and care about the impact that our behaviour has on other people. It makes us able to welcome feedback about our behaviour towards others and adjust it accordingly.

By contrast, narcissists who have an impaired PFC are *unable* to see how their behaviour impacts on others, or care about it. Like small children, they are predominantly limbic. They can only see themselves and their own needs in all situations, and all relationships. The permanent absence of empathy means that they do not experience others as separate human beings who are equally valuable to themselves. What is OK for children and young people while they are in development, is not OK for adults. Adults who do not recognise the impact they have on others and who do not care about it are in fact abusive, and can cause a great deal of harm to others.

One of the ways to define abuse is 'the use of others without their informed consent'. Abuse is only possible where there is an imbalance of power. Where there is an imbalance of power, victims are not in a position to give consent to being used for the abuser's purpose, whatever it might be. Some work arrangements, for example, can be inherently abusive. Any creature exploited without their consent would suffer enormous psychological damage. Only people whose PFC is impaired can be unconcerned about the damage they cause others.

Where the PFC is in charge, abuse is not possible. Anyone with a functional PFC would never use their power to exploit another creature, human or non-human. That is because they naturally grasp the impact they have on others, *and* they care about it. If a person with a functional PFC makes a mistake, they would aim to make amends and learn from it so they never repeat it. Abuse is not a one-off occurrence. It is usually a pattern of behaviour that is consistent, and persistent over time.

Inclusiveness – Our limbic brain is tribal. It cares more about our own group, the people we believe are more likely to look after us and keep us alive. We care more about our close family, group of friends, our community, our nation. We can see this tribalism play out in the way football fans treat the fans of a rival team. Tribalism might be the cause of racism, which is our tendency to prefer the group with which we associate ourselves, and hate or fear the members of other groups.

By contrast, the prefrontal cortex makes us see *everyone* as equally valuable as ourselves, and the members of our groups or communities. Equality does not mean sameness. Equality means that we see everyone as having equal value. It does not mean that everyone is identical, or has exactly the same abilities or needs. Our PFC values difference and sees it as a source of enrichment and growth, not a threat.

If we all acted out of our PFC there would be no racism. Wars would not exist, and we would all be naturally motivated to share our resources for everyone's benefit.

Presence – Presence is the ability to be fully 'there' in a particular moment for someone else without being motivated by our own needs. We make a conscious choice to be present for others. Most psychotherapists know that presence is crucial for therapy to be effective, and they do their best to offer this to clients. We know that being present for someone else has an incredibly healing effect. How well any of us can do this depends on our ability to operate reliably from our PFC.

Presence makes us *safer* for others, especially for children and young people. This is because we are not *caught up* in our own limbic world, our 'agenda', our needs or fears, or our pre-wired assumptions about other people. Presence is unconditional. It allows others to feel *seen* and *noticed* fully and accurately.

For me, presence is linked with attunement. Our PFC allows us to be properly attuned to someone else, notice how they are as a whole being and let them know that we see them.

When we are present, we are also there for ourselves. We are aware of what we feel and experience, and are grounded and peaceful at the same time. I think of it is a state of full consciousness.

Identity and sense of self – This is about our sense of uniqueness, of our individuality. Our PFC tells us that we have unique contributions that only we can make. No one has our voice, our perspective, our ways of feeling and thinking, our abilities, our visions, our imagination, or anything else that makes us who we are. We are aware of the role that only we can play in the world, because there is no one else who is exactly like us.

It is not the same as narcissism, which involves feeling 'special', 'better than', and *deserving* of special treatment. Rather, it is a simple and grounded recognition of our uniqueness, at the same time as knowing that everyone else is also unique, and that and we are not more important or deserving.

The limbic brain's sense of identity is fickle. How we behave, how we would show ourselves in the world would shift and change depending on who we are with, and how safe or unsafe we feel.

Children, who are predominantly limbic, do not have a strong sense of self. They do their best to adapt to their environment to maximise their chances of survival. In the limbic brain we have a drive to be accepted by our group, (or else we risk being tossed out of the cave to die of hunger in the ice age...) If what the group demands is to be quiet and agree with the leader, that is what the limbic brain will do for the purpose of self-preservation. The antelope that looks and behaves like all the other antelopes, and stands in the middle of the herd is less likely to be caught up by a lion than the one that is too curious, and independent minded, and goes exploring by itself.

The sense of identity provided by the PFC seems to be more solid and consistent across situations. We are authentically who we are wherever we are, in any situation, and no matter who we are with. We do not change our behaviour or say things just to fit in with others, or to have our needs met. With the PFC in charge, we are always ourselves. Our behaviour will remain principled, even when we are under threat. 'Groupthink', peer pressure, mob behaviour, etc., are only possible when people's limbic brain is in charge.

Clarity – From the prefrontal cortex our thinking seems to be clearer and 'crisper'. We just *know* what we know, and feel quietly calm about it. We can communicate what we think clearly and quietly without emotional intensity, without justifying ourselves, or making a 'case for ourselves'. We have no need to make others think or believe the same as we do. We can also be clear about being wrong, or ignorant without an emotional reaction.

The capacity for imagination beyond our experience — The limbic brain's imagination is limited by its pre-wired experience. When we make decisions from our limbic brain, we often recreate what we know. The limbic brain does not know what is possible beyond what is already wired into it, or in other words, what it has previously experienced. What we see in the reality around us is what our wiring would let us see.

If we were brought up in a harsh and hostile environment, and this is what was wired in, that is also what we would see around us later in life. Kindness and gentleness are also present in the environment, but would be unfamiliar, and alien to us. Our wiring would make us focus on what it recognises, and ignore what we do not.

We are terrible scientists when our limbic brain is in charge. We look at our reality selectively, and focus on what we already believe (what is pre-wired). This is called 'confirmation bias', which means seeing what we expect to see. Proper scientific method is supposed to counter this. This would have had an important evolutionary purpose, otherwise it would not be there. But in our present reality, it is a serious limitation.

A well-developed prefrontal cortex gives us the ability to imagine 'the impossible', the 'unimaginable', see possibilities that appear beyond reach. We can imagine and visualise things that we have never experienced. It also gives us the drive and creativity to fulfil a seemingly impossible vision.

If, as a species, we want to experience world peace, if we want kindness, abundance, and compassion as the guiding principles for our societies, we have to rely on PFC imagination.

Politics of the 'possible', 'realpolitik', is a surrender to our limbic instincts. It says that there is no point aspiring for anything new, better, or different, and nothing ever changes. We need to stick to what we know, and what we believe is possible. This leads to an unimaginative existence, where we risk perpetuating patterns and conditions that do not serve us. But they are familiar, so no matter how bad they might feel, to our limbic brain they also feel safe.

It is obvious to me that at the moment, as a species, we are making largely limbic, fear-based, short-sighted decisions. Even when faced with the stark reality of climate change, politicians still make decisions based on old ways of doing things.

We cannot see beyond our experience. We cannot imagine a world without war, without vicious competition over resources, without corruption, danger, injustice, or suffering, and without a chronic gap between the 'haves' and the 'have-nots'. We evolved in a harsh and competitive, unforgiving, and indiscriminatory natural environment. It is possible that it is somehow embedded in our collective species' memory. We have so much more control over our environment, and are no longer at the mercy of completely arbitrary natural conditions. Still, we seem unable to stop recreating that harsh world, and we keep reliving it. What we do as individuals, we also do as a species.

The limbic brain might yearn and hope for peace, justice, safety, abundance and happiness, but it cannot make it happen. It does not know how to create something it has not already experienced (i.e., that is wired in). It *cannot imagine* anything beyond its actual experience. Anything different can feel like an unattainable fantasy. It is one of the reasons that recovery from childhood trauma can be so challenging. If we were born into trauma, we cannot imagine anything different. Recovery often involves walking into the unknown and unfamiliar.

People who are driven by limbic instincts often ridicule those who have visions for a better, or different world. Only our PFC can imagine something beyond our experience, and create it. Left to its own devices, our limbic brain can only repeat what it knows.

So, What is Our Problem?

Most people have a fully functional executive brain, with such wonderful abilities. If we are all naturally good, insightful, present and compassionate, then why is the world in such a mess, and why do so many people suffer from 'mental health' problems? Why are people so competitive, and why is there so much suffering, fighting and chaos in the world?

The answer is that unlike our reptilian and limbic brains, which had hundreds of millions of years to cooperate with one another, our ancient limbic brain, and our much younger executive are not connected as well as they can be. They do not 'talk' to each other very well. This has serious implications for our psychology, our wellbeing, and our ability to fulfil our potential and become everything we can become. The poor connectivity between the executive and the limbic brains has a profound impact on the way we parent children, how we are in relationships, how we develop our political beliefs, the way we run our societies, and a great deal more.

We are born with the *potential* for good integration between our limbic and executive functions. Our brain has in-built potential for the limbic and executive systems to cooperate and work well together, each doing what it is meant to do. We are capable of developing good connections between the two brain systems, but we are *not born* integrated.

When our ancestors were faced with a hungry or angry predator, it probably did not pay off to empathise with the animal, feel compassion for it or think deep philosophical thoughts about the purpose of that moment. It is reasonable to assume that those who felt empathy or engaged in deep philosophical thoughts when they faced a predator, did not survive as well as those whose limbic brain 'kicked in', took over and activated the fight-flight-freeze reactions. Acting out of our ancient limbic instincts in the face of immediate threat, worked better. We are the descendants of those who survived better because their limbic brain took over. We carry their genes. It does not matter that we live now in a very different world to the world they lived in. The moment we feel under threat, our limbic brain does what it has evolved to do and shuts down our executive functions. We do not get them back until the threat is over.

Our limbic brain has done well in terms of survival of our species, if what we mean by 'well' is measured by how many of us there are. The size of our population in world we live in now introduces serious challenges to us as individuals and as societies.

Earlier I explained that feelings are information from our limbic system. Now imagine the limbic brain as similar to the continuously rotating radar that you see in airports. The radar's role is to scan the airspace around the airport and 'notice' anything that is up there, a flock of birds, a storm, aircraft flying too close to each other – anything that could pose a threat to planes in the sky and on the ground. When the radio waves from the radar bounce back from anything that could pose a threat to aircraft, this translates into dots on the radar screens in the air traffic control tower. The air traffic controller knows how to interpret the dots on the radar screen and uses this information to make rational, sound decisions in order to keep the airspace safe.

Our safety in the air depends on the presence and skill of air traffic controllers who must constantly monitor the dots on the radar screen. They must interpret them correctly and make the right decisions. We trust that they pay attention to *all relevant information* received and know the right actions to take in different situations.

Suppose the radar worked perfectly fine, but there was no one in the air traffic control tower to receive the information, interpret it and make good decisions. Our limbic brain is like the radar. It continuously scans inside (our body) and outside (our environment) through our senses. When it encounters something, especially a potential threat, it will try to 'report back' with a feeling, which is information.

When our executive and limbic functions are not well connected, it is like having a good, functional radar that works as it's designed to, but an empty air traffic control tower. Just when we need it the most, when we are threatened, the control tower is empty. There is no one there to receive the information and make good decisions. Most of those who come to therapy or people who experience mental health difficulties have an 'internal airspace' that can feel like it's full of chaos and catastrophe.

I think most, if not all readers, would recognise the moment of being triggered. Trigger is what I call the moment when we are unable to think clearly or make good decisions, when the limbic brain has taken over and is in the driver's seat. When the limbic brain senses a threat, we lose our executive ability to think clearly, to have perspective, to be present or to feel empathy. We lose our sense of ourselves, our identity, our values and can feel 'out of control'. In that moment, we become a frightened and reactive mammal. When the threat is over, we usually regain our access to our executive.

People describe how sometimes they are fully aware of what is happening. They can see that they are saying or doing certain things that they know are wrong, but they still cannot stop themselves. At other times, people only realise what they did or said *after* the trigger has passed. (Who hasn't experienced this? I certainly have, many more times than I can count).

The realisation that we have reacted badly following a trigger, often comes with regret for having said or done something hurtful to someone we care about, or having made a poor decision or choice. People often feel guilty and ashamed for 'losing the plot'. But it is not their fault. If you leave the limbic brain in charge to manage a complex situation, it is like leaving a child in charge. A child or young adult would do their best within their abilities, but they are not equipped to deal with adult complexity. You cannot blame a child for making a mess of things, if there is no adult in charge.

Flipping' Between Brains

When we do not have good integration between the two brains, we risk 'flipping' back and forth between our mammal brain and our executive, our prefrontal cortex. One minute we are mature, logical, grounded, present and empathetic, and the next frightened, angry, confused, lost or withdrawn. Since no one is perfectly integrated, most people experience different degrees of 'flipping back and forth'.

Just about every client who comes to therapy complains about something that has to do with flipping back and forth between the two brains. Below are some examples I have put together to illustrate this point. They are based on real stories, but I have disguised the names, and altered key details so that no one could be identified.

'Sunil', a thoughtful, quietly-spoken postgraduate research biologist who is passionate about his chosen area of study:

"I want to finish my degree, but every time I try to sit down and do my studies, I feel restless and want to escape. My work is giving me the time to do it, and my partner is very supportive, but I feel like I am letting everyone down. When I try to force myself to study and work on my papers, I cannot concentrate and I end up writing rubbish. I feel confused, I cannot concentrate or think clearly and I do not know what to do with myself."

'Jasmin', an executive with a responsible job:

"I'm really good at my work and I love it. Everyone respects me and comes to me for advice, because I can always see things so clearly. I stay calm even when everyone else in the office is stressed. I usually make good decisions that are very good for the organisation, and I am also pretty good with people. But as soon as I get home from work and the kids want my attention, I get angry and I start screaming at them. They do not even have to do very much for me to get like that. They do not have to do anything… If people at work could see how I am at home, they would not believe it… I'm embarrassed and I cannot understand myself! How can I be like this? Something must be very wrong with me. I think I am a fraud. I do not like screaming at my kids. I can see that I am destroying their confidence and they look so hurt. When they stay away from me it makes me so sad but I only have myself to blame. I tried everything but it still happens and I cannot help myself, which is why I thought I should try to get some help now. My kids are growing up. I am running out of time, and I am scared of what I am doing to them. I'm scared I'm a terrible mother."

'Siobhan', a retired nurse who has joined a Bible study group:

"Logically I can see that this group is not for me and that I should leave. The people are cold and they do not feel genuine. When I try to talk about the things I'm not happy with in the group, I'm told it's all about my perception and that I should pray more for God's guidance. I'm told that if I just read the Bible more I'd find all the answers I need. In my heart I know what I am seeing is true, and I know that this environment is not good for me. But there is another part of me that doesn't want to upset people, and I do not want to be alone. I'm scared that I'm not a good Christian and that I am too judgmental of people and not a very nice person. So, I stick with it and then feel angry and depressed when I come home from these meetings. This is supposed to be a nice experience that makes my life better, but instead it's just giving me more stress and anxiety."

'Jo', the owner of a successful and busy construction company, originally from a poor family:

"I know I should be proud of myself for what I have achieved. I come from nothing, and am now the owner of this big company and employ a lot of people. I try to be fair to the people who work for me and I look after them. I feel good at work most of the time, and logically I know I am good at what I do. I understand things because I started from the bottom and worked as a builder myself for many years. Even now I don't just sit in the office. I don't enjoy sitting behind a desk. I like to be outside, get my hands dirty, do real work. But there is a part of me that doesn't feel that I deserve the money I have and feels like a child. I feel like a fraud, and I go and drink until I get drunk.

I know this hurts my family, but I can't help myself. I get into these dark moods, and it's getting harder to come out of them. I hate feeling like this. When I try not to drink, I end up eating rubbish and so now I am heavy, and I don't like myself. I've put on a lot of weight in the last few months. I don't sleep so well. I wake up a few times in the night and my head's spinning with worries. Why can't I just be grateful for what I have? So many of the people I grew up with aren't so lucky. I have so much to be grateful for, but thinking like this I feel even more anxious. I probably shouldn't even be here. There are people who deserve therapy much more than I do..."

Many readers and therapists would probably recognise, and relate to the stories above or to some version of them. That inner tension, this inner contradiction within us is real. We are not imagining it. We do have two *ways of being* inside our head, and they are not naturally well integrated.

Interpersonal Neurobiology tells us that we can look at all psychological problems and conditions from the point of view of neural integration. The worse the integration, the more problems people are likely to have. When we are not well integrated and the limbic brain is in charge too much of the time, it will try to perform tasks that it's not equipped or suited for. The limbic brain is made for identifying danger and alerting us to it. It is a brain that has developed in a world very different from the one we live in now that was probably a lot simpler, closer to nature and more straightforward. It is not made to function in the complex world that we have created with our big and ingenious modern brain.[23]

As we grow towards adulthood the demands on us become increasingly complex and our levels of responsibility go up. If the limbic

---

[23] I am not surprised that anxiety is generally on the increase everywhere. The more our technology advances, the more complex our world becomes, the more overwhelmed and perplexed our limbic brain feels. It just is not made for this kind of complexity.

brain is still in charge by the time we are adult, it is going to buckle under the pressure and feel overwhelmed, no matter how intelligent, competent or educated we are. We are likely to feel like a fraud, like children pretending to be adults and we are likely also to be self-critical. Working from our limbic brain is like sending a young child to do the work of an adult and to make them carry an inappropriate level of responsibility.

In the diagram below, I (roughly) illustrate what stress levels can look like relative to levels of responsibility, given different levels of integration. At low levels of integration, stress levels are likely to increase dramatically as people are expected to take more responsibility. We all experience a rise in our levels of responsibility as we grow into adulthood. At medium levels of integration, the levels of stress are lower but are can still be significant as responsibility rises. People with good levels of integration will be able to face increasing levels of responsibility without suffering much stress. Stress will probably plateau at some point.

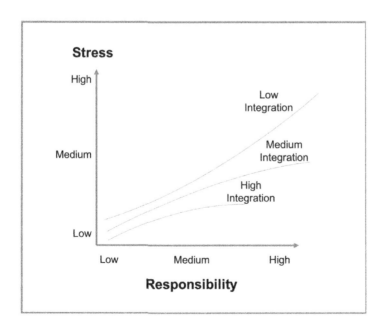

Neural Integration & Its Outcomes

"I have come to prize each emerging facet of my experience, of myself. I would like to treasure the feelings of anger and tenderness and shame and hurt and love and anxiety and giving and fear—all the positive and negative reactions that crop up. I would like to treasure the ideas that emerge - foolish, creative, bizarre, sound, trivial—all part of me. I like the behavioural impulses - appropriate, crazy, achievement-oriented, sexual, murderous. I want to accept all of these feelings, ideas and impulses as an enriching part of me. I do not expect to act on all of them, but when I accept them all, I can be more real; my behavior, therefore, will be much more appropriate to the immediate situation." – **Carl Rogers, A Way of Being**.

What Carl Rogers describes here is his ability to be aware of his feelings, listen to them and accept them without rejecting them. He observes that because he does this, his behaviour has evolved to be 'more appropriate to the immediate situation'. What Rogers is talking about is what happens when we integrate our executive with our limbic functions.

In order to change we need to make changes to our neural architecture. This means that we need to make changes to *connectivity* between different parts of the brain. Connectivity is the way different parts of the brain are wired to each other and 'talk' to each other. Better connectivity means better and more reliable communication between different parts of the brain. Better communication allows us to function better, learn better and respond better to situations.

As I mentioned earlier, we change our neural architecture every time we learn something new. The more we practise, the better we wire things in. The phrase 'practice makes perfect' is true, and we all know this from our experience. Practice 'makes perfect' because practice means repetition and repetition makes neurones fire together in regular and reliable patterns. The more we repeat something, a tune or a song, a hand or body movement, a process for solving a math equation, a new language, operating a tool, a new procedure at work, using a new app or anything at all, the more established and reliable the neural connections become and the better our chances of making them permanent.

It is when neural connections become permanent and fire reliably, that we feel like we are no longer just learners or amateurs, but are more skilled at and confident in what we are doing. As we learn, as we wire in the new knowledge or skill, we move from being slow, tentative, unsure or unreliable to being masterful and at ease with what we have learned. The more established our neural connections and networks become, the more easily, quickly and naturally we can access the skill or knowledge we have acquired. Anything that is well wired, feels like an instinct. We do not have to think about it, we just know how to do something.

One of the most important lessons we learn from Interpersonal Neurobiology (IPNB) is that most of what makes us who and what we are is wired in from our environment. Whatever genetic potential we are born with, how each of us turns out, and whether or not we will fulfil our potential and feel alive and healthy, depends largely on the environment.

The ability of our brain to change its physical structure, its 'architecture', to form new connections between brain cells from different brain regions and establish new neural networks is called 'neuroplasticity'. It is thanks to our neuroplasticity that we are all lifelong learners. In fact, 'learning' means forming neural connections and neural networks in the brain. Without neuroplasticity there is no learning and no change.

Do you remember learning the language that is your first language, or your 'mother tongue'? I was born and raised in Israel and therefore it was Hebrew that was wired into the language centre of my brain. Hebrew was automatically and effortlessly (or at least I was not aware of the effort of learning it) wired in simply from hearing it spoken and repeated all around me. I have no memory of learning it. It went into my head by 'osmosis'. My brain just 'soaked' it in, which means that the environment *caused* my brain to wire it in. When I was ten years-old I started to learn English at school. I do not remember learning Hebrew but I remember learning English. Learning English was something that I did consciously. I was aware of the work and effort I had to put into learning it.

Human beings are born with a brain that is language-ready but we do not have language yet when we are born. We need the environment to wire a language into our brain. If you raise a child in a vacuum where no one speaks, the child will not learn to speak a language.

In a similar way, we are born with a brain that is ready for integration between our limbic and executive functions. But unless the environment provides us with the correct input (as it does with language and everything else we learn in childhood) the connections will not form.

better integration between our limbic and executive functions is at the heart of what we think of as good mental health. It is also associated with feeling that we are growing towards our potential. Dan Siegel argues that our brain, like any complex system, has an innate drive to become more complex. In other words, our brains want to integrate and will always seek opportunities to achieve greater complexity.

Every time we add neural connections to our brain in a significant way, it feels tiring, even exhausting. When we change the architecture of our brain, we are doing something physical that requires actual effort. We do not have the option of putting our brain in a box while it's integrating and using a spare brain for everything else. We continue to use the same brain that is busy integrating to do everything else we need it to do.

Just maintaining our enormous human brain requires about 25% of our energy on a regular basis. When we deliberately set out to make changes to our brain – such as when we embark on learning something new or when we start therapy – it's going to feel exhausting. Think about the last time you learned something new, how tired you felt while you were practicing or absorbing (wiring) new information. You might also recall how, along the way, it got less tiring until you got better at whatever it was you were learning.

It is to be expected that during therapy and throughout the therapeutic process, people will, on and off, feel absolutely 'knackered'. This is especially so when people work to recover from something difficult like childhood trauma. By 'knackered' I mean totally exhausted. It's that feeling that no matter how much or how well you sleep (if you are able to sleep while your brain is so busy) you wake up in the morning feeling like you were hit by a truck…

Each *psychotherapy* modality or approach has its own idea of the goals that it would like to help clients achieve. All the goals that the different approaches aspire to and work towards are compatible with what we achieve with better integration. In other words, all good, effective therapy approaches ultimately strive to help clients integrate their brains better, they just do not necessarily say it like this.

New clients often tell me that they have been to therapy before and that it helped a little at the time, but that the original problems eventually returned. This tells me that perhaps they got some support and comfort at the time, but that no significant neural integration took place. When psychotherapy is effective, the changes are not 'cosmetic' or short-term, but are life-changing and permanent.

If therapy (integration) has been effective, people should experience:

- Significantly reduced anxiety
- Faster recovery from familiar triggers
- Less triggers
- Better boundaries
- A stronger sense of identity, sometimes even a sense that they have a new identity, that is to some degree different to how they were before
- Increase in flexibility and reduction in rigidity
- Ability to make better choices in response to either new, or old and familiar situations
- A sense of 'flowing' better with situations and with life in general; a sense of living with more balance and harmony
- Improved presence and functioning in all relationships
- Increased clarity about which relationships might be appropriate and which might need to be left behind
- Improved ability to make hard choices without inner turmoil
- Increased compassion and empathy towards others and towards themselves as well as a tendency to be less judgemental of others
- Increased sense of personal power
- Increase in confidence

- Improved resilience – that is the ability to bounce back and regain perspective and equilibrium when difficult things happen
- Greater ease and confidence in performing tasks that previously might have felt difficult, such as parenting or leadership roles
- A sense of inner peace, which means much less internal fighting and turmoil
- Increased ability to just relax or be in the moment and enjoy life
- A sense of authenticity, feeling and being real and comfortable in your own skin – as opposed to feeling like a 'fraud' or like a child
- A clearer sense of purpose and direction
- Some people experience more developed and mature spirituality, or at least a new openness to it. People who are part of a faith tend to feel more connected to the divine more of the time. They do not lose this connection as often as previously.

Psychotherapy (see diagram below) should include two stages. Stage one is *vertical integration* and stage two is *horizontal integration*. If approached with attention to these stages, therapy will be safe and people will be able to access what we think of as 'self-support' in order to 'heal' and reintegrate 'unfinished business', hurts from the past, or anything else that is not integrated and continues to cause problems.

If therapists work within this framework they will not cause clients to open up about things prematurely. It is a way of working with the client's brain rather than on therapists' idea of where clients are at or what they need to look at or talk about at different stages of the therapy process. In this framework, the client is well and truly in charge of their own therapeutic process. There cannot be situations when clients go home after a session to try to continue to function with an open 'can of worms' and their 'guts' exposed. When horizontal integration is allowed to begin naturally, people usually feel solid and grounded, even after working to integrate something difficult.

Safe & Effective Psychotherapeutic Process
(With a therapist or DIY)

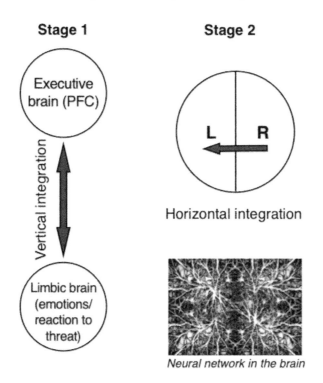

Stage 1

Executive brain (PFC)

Vertical integration

Limbic brain (emotions/ reaction to threat)

Stage 2

L   R

Horizontal integration

Neural network in the brain

Vertical integration — Should be the focus at the start of therapy.

Horizontal integration — Will start naturally when enough vertical integration has been achieved.

Vertical Integration

When we achieve better vertical integration between our limbic and our executive functions, both brains continue do the job they are meant to do but they are much better connected. They remain what they are, each responsible for their respective functions, but information can flow more freely and regularly between them without interruption.

One of the most important outcomes of vertical integration is that the limbic brain can no longer shut down the executive, even when it is triggered in a moment of threat. In other words, when you are better integrated, no matter what you feel, you will not 'lose yourself'. You will be able to feel everything because your limbic brain will continue to work as it is supposed to. But since your executive will also continue to function, you will be fully aware of the information coming from your limbic brain; you will be able to listen to it, soothe it and reassure it and you will then be able to make good decisions based on your executive.

Even if someone's presence or behaviour trigger you, you will not lose your ability to be present and empathetic. You will take care of yourself first and then attend to the outside world. This is precisely what we associate with maturity and with being 'grounded', except this is real, as opposed to pretending to be 'grown-up' from the perspective of our limbic brain but knowing deep down that we are 'faking it'.

If parents handle their children's feelings (information from the child's limbic system) correctly, and can parent mostly from *their* prefrontal cortex, this would directly lead to integration in their children's brain. When the parents' prefrontal cortex receives the information from the child's limbic brain correctly, the child's own two brains will form physical connections naturally. It will be like learning your mother's tongue. It just gets wired in. Children can then grow into adults with better integrated brains naturally (One of my clients once calls it 'Human Mark II'). Since most of our psychological problems are caused by poor integration, the more integrated people are from childhood, the less need there will be for therapy or therapists. This is how I hope to make myself redundant.

If no one ever did any of this for you when you were a child, your prefrontal cortex will not have been 'trained' to 'speak' to your limbic brain properly. In other words, you will not have good connections between the brains. This means that information from your limbic brain does not flow reliably into your prefrontal cortex. You are then more likely to find yourself 'lost' when you are triggered by something, and caught up in your feelings and fears without the ability to look after yourself, ground yourself, feel safe, think clearly or make good choices.

You do not have to have been neglected or abused in order to grow up with poor vertical integration. This is simply the developmental stage of our species. Our parents and their parents and those who came before them didn't know what they didn't know. But we know better now. Abusing and neglecting children is obviously unacceptable and it often leads to trauma. Trauma is a severe and unfair extra burden on people that can rob them of the opportunity to develop, of enjoying good physical health. It can robe people even of life itself given that childhood trauma can lead to suicide and addictions. But regardless of what your childhood was like, everyone needs to integrate better.

Even if your childhood was OK, if you are not well integrated, you are likely to have problems. No one can fulfil their potential or feel at peace internally if their two brains are not well-integrated. To achieve better vertical integration, we need to *train* the PFC to attend to information coming from the limbic brain and receive it properly and correctly. This has the effect of increasing the connections and ultimately allowing information from the limbic brain to flow freely to the executive. Therapy does not start with people talking about all the worst things that ever happened to them. It should start with a targeted approach to training the prefrontal cortex to do something it may not have been trained to do in childhood.

This is different from traditional psychotherapy approaches. Other approaches, without even realising it, assume that somehow the interaction between the client and the therapist will lead to spontaneous changes in the client's brain. In the approach I use, and that I teach here, we no longer leave it to chance. Clients know exactly what they are supposed to do, and my job is to help them do it.

Because my clients are adults, I cannot integrate their brains for them.[24] In teaching my clients to work on their vertical integration, I see my role closer to that of a guide, a companion on the journey and

---

[24] Anyone who works with children can integrate their brains directly from the outside. But adults have to do the hard work themselves. It's like learning a language as adults compared with learning it naturally and without awareness of effort because it was spoken in our childhood environment.

96

hopefully a decent enough role model. My role is also to be a facilitator who provides an environment that is supportive of this therapeutic work.

Everything I have ever learned about fostering a good therapeutic relationship with my clients – it's called a 'therapeutic alliance' – is all valid and useful. No client would ever listen to me or engage in this work if they didn't feel comfortable with me or perceive me as trustworthy or credible. Clients cannot achieve much with a therapist they do not trust or feel safe with. Therapists do have an important role to play but the real work depends on what clients do between sessions. There is nothing magical about seeing me or any therapist. Integration is achieved from the work that clients do between sessions.

I never dictate to my clients how often to see me because everyone is different. Everyone's brains have different things wired into them and integrative work happens at different speeds. People have different life circumstances, availability, commitments such as children and childcare and financial considerations that can be important factors in deciding when and how often to attend therapy sessions. There is no clinical evidence that any length of time between sessions, or the overall number of sessions, has any relevance to what we call 'therapeutic outcome'. Everyone is different. I leave it to my clients to decide how often and how much to see me, and they all know I work for them and not the other way around.

The exercise that follows is what all my clients are doing when they first start therapy with me. I have a bookmark in the Resources section on my website. It includes a 'reminder' of this practice, and you are welcome to download it from there.

Vertical Integration Exercise

Step 1 — Accessing the prefrontal cortex (PFC)

Accessing the prefrontal cortex is a crucial part of the process that is worth taking time for. Integration can only be achieved when the PFC is engaged. Most people's PFC works instinctively and often. But to integrate it with our limbic functions we need to develop mastery. In other words, we need to learn to activate the PFC by choice rather than wait for it to happen by chance.

You will not achieve integration if your limbic brain takes over and tries to do the exercise. This will be the equivalent of a child trying to look after his or her own emotions, which is what you probably had to do in your early years anyway. This did not lead to integration, only to your limbic brain learning to cope.

For integration in childhood, we need the correct relationship between an adult and a child. What we do in this exercise is simulate the correct relationship inside our own brain in order to achieve the same result. (We are fortunate to have neuroplasticity so we can do it at any age. We do not have to remain stuck for the rest of our lives with the brain we had when we left our childhood home).

Many years ago I learned breathing practices in yoga classes. These practices had different purposes. One of the exercises I learned was specifically intended to 'awaken the third eye' or the 'observer', as our wise yoga teacher called it. The exercise involved breathing 'into' the eyebrow centre in a particular way and focusing our *attention* there. Building on this and other practices I have learned over the years, I have developed this exercise that I teach all my clients.

I know you have to read the instructions to do the exercise, and you cannot read and do it at the same time. I suggest you read the whole practice first until you feel you remember enough to attempt it, and do your best. After a few repetitions, you will remember it easily because you will have wired in the instructions. Another suggestion is to record the instructions in your own, or someone else's voice and play the recording as you would with any meditation tape.

It is hard to suggest a timeframe for this work because everyone's different. The principle is that the more times you do this, the quicker you will integrate. If you decide to follow this exercise, I suggest you try

98

to set aside 15-20 minutes for it. Feel free to take more or less time as you need or as you are able to.

Try to choose somewhere quiet where you will not be interrupted. Some people find it helpful to do this as soon as they wake up in the morning while they are still in bed, or as the last thing they do before they fall asleep at night or both. Think of it as learning to say 'good-morning' or 'goodnight' to yourself.

People who like structure and planning their time, prefer to schedule specific times for this. People who do not like timetables do this when it feels right. You know yourself better than anyone and you need to do what comes more naturally to you.

As your brain integrates you will no longer need to follow the exercise in a structured form. The connections between your brains will change how you are and you will know when it begins to happen. As your connections grow, you will do this all the time without thinking, even while washing dishes or sitting in a meeting at work. Integration simply means that the information between your limbic and executive brains will be flowing back and forth without interruption as it does in other parts of your brain.

Accessing your PFC

1. Find a comfortable place to sit or lie down. (It is important to be comfortable because any discomfort in the body will trigger the limbic brain and it will attempt to take over. There is no point in being uncomfortable physically).

2. Cast your eyes to the farthest part of the room or space you are in

3. Bring your eyes to the middle of the room

4. Bring your eyes to about reading distance

5. Now draw your attention to your nostrils. Notice how the air goes in and out of your nostrils. You might notice a slightly cool sensation as the air enters your nose and a slightly warm and moist sensation when the air comes out. Do this for a few moments.

6. Now draw your attention to your chest. Notice how it expands when you breathe in and then contracts when you breathe out. Do this for a few moments.

7. Now draw your attention to your abdomen. Notice how your tummy expands when you breathe in and how it contracts when you breathe out. Do this for a few moments.

8. Join your awareness of the nose, chest and abdomen. Become curious about your breath and follow it with your mind. Nose – chest – abdomen – abdomen – chest – nose. Do this for a few moments.

9. In your next inhalation, with awareness and attention, draw your breath all the way up to your forehead and imagine that you can fill it up with air. Give it a little time and see what that feels like. Do you feel anything in your forehead? Is there a sensation there? Do you see something? An image, a colour, a shape? Do you perhaps hear something? Do not try to make anything happen. Just breathe into the forehead, and let your brain do the rest. Where our attention and breath go, our neurones fire. Do not look for anything in particular. This is an exercise in paying attention.

10. Whatever you experience in your forehead as you breathe into it, feed it gently with more air and oxygen and allow the sensation or image to develop even more. There is no right or wrong, everyone is different so every person sees or experiences something different. Often what you experience or see might change each time you do this, so do not try to bring up the same image or sensation you had the previous time. Trust your brain – it knows what to do. All you need to do is pay attention to the breath and extend it to the forehead.

Other suggestions to help you access the prefrontal cortex

• If you are used to meditating, or to breathing practices, or yoga, if you listen to a meditation or relaxation tape or practice mindfulness, you can use this as a way to access your prefrontal cortex. Studies have shown that meditation and breathing practices cause the neurones in the prefrontal cortex to fire, which is what we want. The exercise above is one suggestion in case you are not familiar with other practices. But if you already have a practice, use it.

- Another way to gain access to the prefrontal cortex is to recall a moment or situation from your life when you did something in a way that felt perfect. You were calm, comfortable in your skin, you didn't feel much, but you knew how to do what you were supposed to do, your thoughts were crystal clear. You were quietly confident and whatever it was you had to do felt easy and effortless. Maybe it was a moment of excellent parenting, or an experience at work, or a perfect moment with a friend or another person when you responded to the situation perfectly and just knew what was needed and how to be.

Remember that what we are trying to achieve is mastery. We want to access the PFC when *we choose to*, not leave it to chance. So, if you know you are likely to be in your PFC in certain situations in your life, it helps to bring yourself to that state by just thinking about being in that situation or in that role. Some of my clients call it 'parent mode', grandparent, nurse, doctor, teacher or manager 'mode'.

How to know if you succeeded in accessing your prefrontal cortex

- You will not feel much at first
- You will feel more present and more comfortable in your body
- Your thoughts will be clear
- You will feel a sense of rightness about the present moment, that feeling that things are exactly as they're supposed to be and that it is fine

Challenges to accessing the prefrontal cortex

It can be difficult to get access to your PFC if you are grieving, if you are hormonal or if you are tired or unwell. It is especially hard if you are already flooded with strong emotions and are in the middle of a big trigger. People who suffer from trauma and are regularly flooded, can find this especially difficult and it can take time to master. It's not your fault! It's our nature. Take your time.

Remember that the mammal brain has evolved to shut down our higher functions when it feels threatened. If the limbic brain already thinks there is a bear in front of us, then to breathe in and not act on our fear but do this exercise can feel like madness to the limbic brain. It might feel something like, 'You want me to relax when there is a bear in front of us? Have you lost your mind?'

The answer of course is to breathe and validate this very feeling. If you can, tell your limbic brain that you are not trying to relax it, all you want to do is to listen to what it has to say. If it says it feels under threat, then this is the information that it is trying to communicate. (I never said it was easy!)

My experience was very much like this in my younger years when my brain was still full of trauma. When I tried to engage in yoga and relaxation, each time I tried to breathe and relax I ended up in a panic. But remember, this is *not* a relaxation exercise and we are *not* asking the limbic brain to do anything. The exercise is meant to give you conscious access to your executive functions so you can begin to receive the information that your limbic brain is trying to communicate (see Step 2 below).

Even if all you manage is a few seconds of access, this can be enough to complete the process. If you find it too difficult, stop, rest and try again another time.

Step 2 — Becoming aware of the limbic brain

1. **Turning your awareness inwards:** While your attention is drawn to your forehead and you are feeding it with your breath, gently turn your awareness to your body and to your emotions. The PFC is a natural observer both of the outside and the inside, including the body. At this point you are learning to turn your conscious attention to the inside, to your limbic activity, by choice.

2. **Noticing your feelings:** Some people find it fairly easy to identify what they are feeling. They might feel irritated, impatient, anxious (afraid), happy or relaxed and they know they are feeling it. Their limbic brain 'speaks' clearly.

3. **Noticing your thoughts:** Sometimes feelings are not clear and what we get instead are thoughts. But there are always feelings behind the thoughts.

   For example, if you hear yourself think 'That's a whole lot of nonsense and how is this going to help me?', perhaps the feeling behind it is of fear that it won't work, or impatience, or even anger or frustration.

   You might hear yourself think, 'Am I doing it right?' The feeling behind this could be fear from the limbic brain, because it thinks it's supposed to do something complicated and it does not know how.

4. **Noticing your body:** Sometimes emotions are not clear at all and when you try to listen to your limbic brain you do not 'hear' anything. It's like you just do not know what you are feeling. This experience is quite common for people who grew up in an environment where they had to hide their emotions for whatever reason, people who grew up in ultra-rational environments where feeling and expressing emotions were discouraged in some way, or if they were not given the opportunity to have any emotional connection with the adults around them.

   If you find it difficult to notice what you are feeling, it is important then to begin to observe your body. Once you have accessed your prefrontal cortex, begin to notice what is going on in your body. Do you notice any energy anywhere, any tiredness, tension, movement, itchiness, pain? Whatever you notice, ask yourself what that body part would be saying if it had a mouth to speak. This will gradually reveal your feelings. You might be surprised by what your body will 'tell' you about what you might be feeling.

   For example, if you feel a tightness in your shoulders, ask yourself what would the shoulders say if they had a mouth to speak. If you notice a movement in your foot or your hands, a sensation in your abdomen, your throat, your neck, ask the same question. The answer to the question will tell you how you feel.

   I have learned this principle of allowing body parts to 'speak' in my Gestalt therapy training. Body and mind are not separate.

Everything about us is a part of one complex system that is interconnected and has its own wisdom.

5. While you are paying attention to what your limbic brain is communicating through feelings, thoughts or body sensations, make sure you check in with your forehead regularly and that you maintain the image, sensation or sound that you are sensing there.

Step 3 — Interacting with the limbic brain

As your PFC becomes aware of the activity in your limbic brain (thoughts, feelings, body sensations) you need to tell it three things:

1) **Whatever *you* are feeling is OK** – Acknowledging and v*alidating* everything your limbic brain is telling you it is feeling *including pleasant feelings*. All feelings, pleasant or uncomfortable are communication from the limbic brain.

2) **I am here** – *Soothing* your limbic brain

3) **Everything's going to be OK** – *Reassuring* your limbic brain

Every time you do this, integrative fibres will grow between the brains. The more you practice, the more they'll grow and the more permanent they will become. Repetition reinforces connections in the brain, just like when we learn anything. Over time you will develop an extensive neural network of connections between the two brains and you will feel different to how you were before.

Tips & Notes

*   **An alternative practice** – If you are not keen on following exercises there is an alternative way to approach this. If you know you are feeling something, just breathe into your forehead and then validate, soothe or reassure your feelings. It will have the same impact. Instead of stopping and waiting for feelings to present themselves, you can use any feeling that arises in your everyday life. To start with, do not try to do this with the most difficult or challenging feelings you have. Try first with simpler and less

powerful feelings. Remember to validate *all* your feelings, not just the uncomfortable ones.

- **Doubts** – If no one has ever validated, soothed and reassured your emotions when you were a child or a teenager, you might experience doubt or rejection from inside you. If you do feel cynical, sullen, resentful or doubtful about the validating message or any part of this practice, you need to recognise that these feelings too come from your limbic brain. All feelings do and it is all just information. Again, validate, soothe and reassure this as well!

You can think of it this way: If I asked you to begin to look after a young person or a child who has not had a particularly great start to life and does not trust adults, how do you think this young person or child would respond to you when you begin to form a relationship with him or her?

The worse the experience was in the child or young person's life, the longer it might take for them to trust you. If a young person or a child responds to your attempts to relate to them with rejection, suspicion or even anger, what do you do? Do you give up? Get angry or impatient with them? Hopefully not, because that would mean that you are acting out of your limbic brain.

If, on the other hand, you act out of your PFC you would know to validate whatever the young person or child feels or says. This is the only way to help them feel that they are in a safe relationship. If they say nothing, or respond with anger or suspicion, you will need to say, 'listen, it's OK not to trust me. You do not know me yet. Whatever you feel right now is OK'.

Younger children tend to develop trust quicker than adolescents. Similarly, parts of your limbic brain might feel more trusting more quickly and others might feel less trusting and more prickly or suspicious. (See the section 'Mapping Your Inner World' later on).

You just have to persist and be consistent. Validate everything as you would be with a real child or young person. If you are able to access your PFC, it won't be difficult to do. Children or young people want to be connected to safe and validating adults because their brain wants to integrate. Your brain is the same. It wants to integrate, so it will eventually respond to you but you have to practice. Just remember, it makes perfect sense that the trickier your history, the longer this will likely, and understandably, take.

It's up to adults to prove themselves to children not the other way around! I always tell my clients that their emotions might have brought them to therapy, but it's their prefrontal cortex that is really in therapy. Because most of us never had good role-modelling for this, we have to learn it now. It is therefore the PFC that has to do all the work, not the limbic brain. The latter has suffered enough already, and, either way, it cannot integrate itself.

- **Speaking to the limbic brain in the second person** – There is a good reason why you should speak to the different parts of yourself in the second person, as 'you' (e.g., 'Whatever *you're* feeling is OK').

When we were children, other people interacted with us using the word 'you' simply because we were separate people. Our brain responds to this language naturally. My experience is that it works far better and more effectively than using 'I'. Children's brains integrate naturally when adults validate the children's limbic emotions. The same happens in the adult brain when the PFC validates emotions, or receives information coming from the person's own limbic brain.

- **Reduction in anxiety** – One of the outcomes of doing this work is a noticeable reduction in anxiety. If, like a lot of people, you suffer from anxiety on a regular basis, you will begin to notice that you begin to feel less anxious. Your levels of anxiety will decrease in general, or you might experience moments when it's gone completely. They might be brief moments at first. If you are used to living with a lot of anxiety, it is likely to feel strange in the beginning. Validate that too.

Anxiety and the adrenaline that drives it are addictive. If you are used to feeling 'hyper' a lot, you might feel like you do not know what to do with yourself when you feel less hyper. You might even feel bored or empty. It will certainly feel unfamiliar. Remember the limbic brain does not like anything new or unfamiliar. It might be naturally suspicious or go back on the alert, especially if you have been used to living with anxiety for a long time.

If/when you notice discomfort, doubt or suspicion about being less anxious, use this same exercise and continue to validate, soothe and reassure. Your limbic brain will eventually get used to living with less anxiety and will in fact welcome it in the long term. The more integration you achieve, the less anxiety you should expect to experience. The less anxiety, the more energy you will free up to use for other things.

- **Recovery time from triggers** – Some hurts and some triggers take longer to heal (integrate), sometimes a lot longer, but their impact diminishes. As your vertical integration improves, recovery time from familiar triggers will also improve. If you normally take a few weeks to recover from something familiar (a strong reaction to a person, or a situation) you might notice you recover in a few days. It might then be reduced to hours or less, until eventually the recovery is almost instantaneous. In the longer term, familiar triggers become less intense and many of them will disappear completely.

- **Writing** – When I started to do this work I found writing helpful. Instead of just having the dialogue in my head, I would write down the 'conversation' I would have with myself. If it works for you, give it a try. Everyone is different so we each have to find our own way. As long as we teach our prefrontal cortex to acknowledge and validate all our emotions, our brain will change.

- **How long does it take?** – The deeper the hurt, the more 'hardwired' it is, so the longer it would take to rewire. But validation of emotions is crucial. Even if you said nothing else, just by telling yourself that what you're feeling is ok, you would know you're not alone. Of course, you could also reassure another person this way.

We (our limbic brains) desperately need to know that we are not alone when we suffer and when we are afraid.

Assessing your progress

Notice your recovery time from familiar triggers – Does it take you the same amount of time to recover as it always has or are you recovering quicker from something familiar?

How long does it take you before you feel you are present again and are able to regain your self-awareness and empathy for yourself and the other people in the situation?

Notice the frequency of familiar triggers – Are you still triggered every single time in the same way you always have been, or are there times when the same situation no longer affects you the same way?

Notice the intensity of the trigger – Does the familiar trigger begin to feel a little less intense than it used to be?

'Hands in the Water' Exercise
(Regulating the flow of energy in the brain)

Before I go into the exercise itself, there are a few things I need to highlight, some of which are mentioned earlier in this book in one form or another. So please bear with me.

In the vertical integration exercise above we focused on the transfer of *information* between the limbic system and the executive brain. We do this by listening to thoughts, feelings, memories, images and even body sensations (you can think of all of these as *information*) communicated from the limbic system, and by responding to them correctly with acknowledgement and validation.

This is not difficult for our prefrontal cortex to do, because it is the part of our brain that gives us the capacity to be naturally non-judgemental, compassionate, inclusive and attuned. The PFC can do this, but it doesn't know how to because we were not taught and didn't see examples of this in our childhood or throughout life.

Enabling a smooth, uninterrupted flow of information between the two brains leads to the creation of solid pathways between them. In other words, it improves the connectivity between the two brains. This changes the structure of our brain permanently, which moves us in the direction of growth and development with the predictable and significant improvement in mental health.

Forming solid and reliable connections between the limbic and executive brains is analogous to creating a solid bond between an adult and a child. If adults knew how to handle children's limbic communication correctly – that is children's emotions and anything else they try to communicate from their limbic brain – and if adults were working to develop better connections in their own brains, children would grow up with better integrated brains naturally. Those of us who were not offered this in our childhoods can achieve better vertical integration later thanks to *neuroplasticity*, the ability of the brain to continually change its architecture. Without neuroplasticity in different parts of the brain there can be no learning or development, people would never adjust to change and no one would ever recover from the impact of brain injury or a stroke. Neuroplasticity is what enables psychotherapy to have an impact at all. If the brain couldn't change, what would be the point of therapy?

The mind ('psyche') is at the heart of psychotherapy but no one knows exactly what the mind is. You cannot dissect a brain and point to where the mind is located because it is not a physical thing like the tissue of the brain. Dr Dan Siegel tentatively defines the mind as a *process* that regulates the flow of energy and information.[25]

When we work on vertical integration by talking to ourselves the right way, we facilitate the *flow of information* between the brains. But what about the *flow of energy*? What about the parts that are wired into our limbic brain from before we had language and before we had the ability to create thoughts (cognition)? In other words, what about our very young selves, our new-born baby selves that are also wired into our limbic system but couldn't speak, form thoughts or understand verbal communication from others? This aspect of ourselves also needs to integrate, and this exercise is intended for this purpose.

Some people were fortunate enough to have been born into a safe environment where the adults instinctively knew how to regulate their baby's brain with the right touch or movement. But many of us were born into dysregulated environments and relationships. If our parents were themselves dysregulated, they didn't know how to regulate us. Even if they did rock us in their arms, we would not have felt soothed because they were internally messy and we felt it. In dysregulated environments children can be exposed to distressing sounds and images of conflict. Even babies or toddlers can be targets of aggression or alternatively of coldness and distance. Sometimes children are not touched at all and are left alone for long periods of time to cry and soothe themselves. People who were not regulated enough early in life can experience anxiety in adulthood, along with the behaviours they develop to cope with it. These behaviours are desperate and unconscious attempts at self-regulation.

This exercise enables communication or flow between the brains that does not require words or thoughts. It is based on what safe adult care givers naturally do when a baby is unsettled, which is hold the baby and rock him or her gently from side to side. That gentle rocking movement is so instinctive, we hardly even think about it. Most of us just know to do it when someone puts a baby in our arms. It's that lovely gentle movement from side to side that soothes babies' brains because

---

[25] See Daniel Siegel's *Mind. A Journey to the Heart of Being Human.*

it helps to regulate them. A regulated brain is a calm brain. Cradles can do it too, but feeling the warmth and heartbeat of a safe person's body against our baby self is the best.

'Hands in the' Water Exercise

1. Please sit or lie comfortably.

2. Close your eyes if you feel comfortable.

3. Bring to your mind a place outdoors where you enjoy being and where you feel safe and free. It can be a real or an imaginary place, a place you saw in a film or read about in a book, a memory from your past, somewhere in your present, or a combination. Give yourself a few moments until an image presents itself.

4. Imagine yourself in that space and allow yourself a few moments to observe and absorb the environment and to feel settled in it. Listen to the sounds around you, notice the sensations in your body, the temperature and feel of the air, the sensations on your skin and under your feet and notice anything your eyes are observing.

5. Find a spot in this space where there is water. Many people seem to have water in the place their mind brings up. But if water is not in there you might need to add it. Please add to the place your mind brought up a calm pond, or a rockpool, or any peaceful body of water that feels right to you.

6. Walk to the water. Imagine yourself sitting comfortably in front of it. Now place your hands in the water as deep as your wrists or a little deeper.

7. Start moving your hands from side to side in a gentle, slow, regular movement. It is the sort of thing a small child might do as they playfully explore water with their hands.

8. Move your hands from side to side gently. Notice the sensation of the water on your skin and between your fingers. Imagine tiny little

fish swimming through your fingers. They do not disturb you and you do not disturb them. Notice the slight resistance of the water and the ease of moving your hands through the water. Notice the subtle, gentle ripples and waves you are creating with the movement.

9. Now extend the sensation to the rest of your body. Allow this gentle side to side movement to extend throughout the whole of your physical body.

10. Now gently allow this sensation to spread upward into your head. Imagine that you are moving your hands in the space between your limbic brain and your prefrontal cortex, from one brain to the other and back again. Gently, gently, move the space from side to side in the same way your hands move in the water.

11. Notice how this makes you feel.

You can incorporate this exercise into your daily life. Once you are comfortable with it, you do not even have to close your eyes. You can bring that sensation into your body and mind just by bringing up the image or sensation of your hands moving in the water. The image of the hands in the water is like an anchor that takes you back to the experience of regulating your own brain.

This is a safe exercise to do. It can help you integrate all the versions of you from the past that are wired into your limbic brain, including the youngest versions of you, before you could speak or think.

Mindfulness Practice & Vertical Integration Work

What is the difference between mindfulness practice or 'loving-kindness' meditation practice and vertical integration work? *Is there a difference?* In principle, there shouldn't be, but there is, and it can be significant. A lot depends on how practices are taught and used and in particular what purpose they are used for.

Mindfulness and meditation were developed as a part of Buddhism. Unfortunately, they are often taught without any connection to their spiritual context or the purpose for which they were originally created. I am sad to see so many therapists and mental health services 'hijacking' mindfulness as just another 'technique' to help people 'relax' or manage anxiety.

When people have trauma, their limbic brain can be triggered into threat a lot of the time. If people with trauma try to practice mindfulness *with the aim of relaxing* they might feel like they are failing. Their limbic brain might resist attempts to breathe differently or relax it. Such exercises can lead to panic and hyperventilation. Integration is not about relaxation and relaxation is not the aim of the exercise.

The idea that everyone should just practice mindfulness or meditation regardless of their psychological state can cause people to feel worse and give up completely. If people are not told that the purpose is not relaxation but integration and that they are supposed to access their PFC, there is a risk they will try to be kind and loving to themselves from their limbic brain. Even if they succeed somehow in being kind to themselves from their limbic brain, the limbic brain *cannot* integrate itself to itself... Our main task for growth and development is to integrate our limbic functions with our executive. But this will not happen if the limbic brain is only talking to itself, it will simply continue to do more of the same, perhaps slightly nicer.

In some approaches to mindfulness or meditation people are told to 'let go' of 'distractions', feelings, thoughts, worries, or even body sensations, as if those take them away from what they are supposed to be doing. But it is precisely all the information from our limbic brain, all the feelings, body sensations and thoughts that are crucial for integration and need to be brought to the front. Far from being distractions, they are information from the limbic brain that is supposed to be received regularly by the executive. We do not want to 'let them go'. If we want to integrate we have to bring them in closer. We must not just brush them off, even with 'loving-kindness'. In fact, brushing feelings or other inner experiences off couldn't be further away from being loving or kind.

Imagine a child coming back from school feeling some kind of distress or unhappiness. Now imagine a calm and non-judgemental parent just standing there quietly, observing the child but doing and saying absolutely nothing. Some of the practices that people are taught look a bit like that. It is a good thing if parents do not judge and do not not interfere with, or try to change how their child feels. But just standing and doing or saying nothing does not contribute to any sense of connection between the adult and the child. It therefore ultimately does not help the child to feel safe or to integrate. What we want inside our head is an ongoing, lively uninterrupted transmission of information between our two brains. We can think of it as the equivalent of a safe and loving relationship between an adult and a child who have an uninterrupted flow between them.

The prefrontal cortex must welcome *everything* that comes from the limbic brain, and I mean everything! It must actively acknowledge (validate) all the information from the limbic brain, however it presents itself, in order to enable this information to move to the front of the brain. It is this activity that enables the uninterrupted flow of information between the two brain systems and the formation of permanent connections between them.

The purpose of the vertical integration process is *not to relax people*, but to integrate them. In fact, more often than not, when the prefrontal cortex makes itself available to the limbic brain, people begin to notice stronger feelings. They might become aware of more suffering and pain inside them rather than less. In a relationship with a real child, our job is not to 'relax' the child but help them feel everything and communicate everything with the knowledge that they are not alone and that they are safe, no matter what. When this is available children feel safe and loved (and they also integrate).

Those among my clients who have been meditating regularly, sometimes for decades, have found that meditation has not changed them much. In particular, their triggers and the suffering they represent, are still there. This is why these clients come to therapy, often wondering what is wrong with them. Being practiced meditators these clients are really good at accessing their PFC. Meditation practice makes the neurons in the PFC fire but it does not automatically integrate the brains. They still need to validate, soothe and reassure all their limbic activity.

Horizontal Integration

Vertical integration is the process of connecting the executive and limbic brains better. Horizontal integration is about linking up the right and left hemispheres. Our right brain is where raw experiences from our history are stored or safely 'quarantined', until they are ready to be 'processed'. Our right brain contains stuff from any time in our history that we haven't yet 'sorted', 'dealt with', 'made sense of', 'come to terms with', 'made peace with', 'healed', etc. We 'suppress' or avoid certain memories, feelings or experiences for as long as it is necessary, that is until it is safe enough to integrate them from right to left.

In this context 'processed' means integrated to the left side of our brain. This is when we finally understand or see something in a new way. It is the process of 'making sense' of experiences, finishing 'unfinished business' or 'resolving' something and 'making peace' with it. What we call 'healing' is in fact horizontal integration.

(I have to take a short but important detour here. Please bear with me. I promise it will all become clear).

The human brain has often been compared to a computer. While there are some superficial similarities, there is not one computer on the planet that can come even close to the human brain. There might never be.

Computers are made of hardware and software that are separate. A computer is just a lump of sophisticated electronic equipment. But without software to make it run it won't do anything useful. Your computer 'comes alive' when the software that's installed in it starts working. The physical computer provides the environment for the software to do what it is programmed to do. Software on its own is also just a bunch of meaningless code ('code' is the word for computer programmes) that can do nothing without being in something that allows it to operate. Software and hardware need each other to become a computer but they are still separate things.

Artificial intelligence (AI) software – which is in all of our computers now and all of our smart devices – can change itself as it learns. It does it by writing new code that wasn't there before. Unlike ordinary

116

software, AI software is not a finished thing once the programmer finished coding (programming) it. It has been created to have the capacity to make changes to itself so that it can do more and be more useful. But no matter how many new lines of code an AI can add to itself, it cannot change the *physical* environment it exists in. The AI software, which runs your email program for example, can learn what email you think is 'junk'. Every time you tell it something is 'junk', you 'teach' it and it changes its own code accordingly. It can then automatically take an email from your Inbox and put it away somewhere else. But it cannot cause the electronic circuitry of your computer to be anything other than what it is. The AI software *cannot change* the physical computer it is operating in.

In the human brain we do not know where the 'hardware' ends and the 'software' begins. What we would call the 'hardware', the actual brain tissue, brain cells and circuitry, and what we might call the 'software', our thoughts and intentions and all the mental activity – our 'mind' – form a *complex system*.

One of the qualities of a complex system is that it is *self-organising*.[26] In our brain it means that the mind, our inner mental activity, has a direct impact on the physical circuitry of our brain and vice versa. As our mind changes, it changes the physical architecture of the brain and as the physical architecture of the brain changes, it changes our mind, how we feel, behave, what we believe, think, want, etc.

If that were not the case, there would be no point in talking about growing and changing, and psychotherapy would be a pointless activity. When you change your mind, that is your feelings, thoughts, behaviours, intentions, hopes, dreams, expectations, values, etc., you are in fact changing the physical architecture of your brain. Our ability to learn and what we call psychotherapy completely depend on it.

Because what we call the mind has the ability to change the architecture of our physical brain, feeling too overwhelmed can in fact 'break' the physical brain. By 'break' I mean cause damage to the physical components, the circuitry and operation of our physical brain. All

---

[26] You can read a great deal more about this and in far more detail in Dan Siegel's wonderful book, *Mind, The Journey to the Heart of Being Human.*

healthy brains protect themselves from this kind of physical harm by quarantining difficult material in the right brain, until the conditions are right and it is safe to integrate them to the left side of the brain.

For example, when a shocking, powerful loss happens, such as losing someone we love in a car crash or to a sudden, unexpected heart attack, most people would tend to feel numb initially. They would feel things more deeply and clearly gradually, over time, but rarely straight away. This numbness, the inability to feel the full force of the shock of the loss in that one moment, is our brain's way of protecting itself from breaking, from actual physical damage.

Most children's brains are good at protecting themselves from physical damage, which is why so many people who have grown up in inadequate environments do make it to adulthood and are perfectly sane. Many people might have difficulties, but their brains are intact and are not permanently 'broken'. They might be traumatised or otherwise in a state of suffering, but they won't have a 'mental illness'.[27]

We know that it is not simply what happens to us that can wound us psychologically. It is usually how we are handled by others when something happens that would determine whether or not we would suffer harm. For example: A six-year-old child attends the funeral of her grandmother. The child loved her grandmother and feels sad, so she cries as the coffin is lowered into the ground. The child's mother notices her cry, she bends and hisses sharply into her ear, "What are you crying about? It's your father who's just lost his mother." *(How are you feeling reading this?)*

In that moment, the child was strictly and sharply prohibited from expressing her sadness in a natural, healthy way. It is likely that this is not the first nor the last time that this child's natural expression of feelings was mishandled. But even if it only happened once (and there

---

[27] I have long suspected that real mental illness, the kind where it seems people cannot get better no matter what might be caused by a lack of sufficient natural defences in the brain. Perhaps as a result of genetic variations, some people's brains are less able to protect themselves from physical harm. Then, when something overwhelming happens, perhaps these people's brains are physically damaged. Once we know even more about the brain and our scanning technology gets more refined, I would like psychiatrists to scan everyone's brain before they arrive at a diagnosis. At the moment a lot of psychiatry and mental health are based on guesswork. It might be correct a lot of the time, but it would be good to be more certain so that people who can change will be offered the opportunity to do so.

was no apology from the mother later[28]) this child would learn a powerful lesson that expressing certain feelings like sadness and grief is wrong, even dangerous. She would learn that she is 'bad' because her crying makes mother angry. She would also learn that by crying she somehow did something to hurt her father.

I have seen many adults who went through similar experiences. Even decades later they would come to therapy suffering from anxiety. They usually have trouble with feeling and expressing grief or sadness, or other feelings that were either treated clumsily by adults, or that went unnoticed so that the child had no help to feel them.

When children go through difficult experiences, all they need is a trusted, attuned, safe adult to validate their feelings, allow them to express them without judgement or criticism, soothe them and keep them safe. Even one adult will do. If this is done close enough to the original experience, the child's right brain will not need to quarantine the experience and it will not become a problem in adulthood. We only quarantine experiences when we do not have help from the outside to 'process' and integrate them close enough to the time of the original experience. When an adult treats a child's feelings correctly, the mind of the adult interacts with the child's mind. Since our mind can change the physical brain, the adult mind helps the child's physical brain develop and integrate, which, in turn, will also affect the child's mind.

Unfortunately, children's feelings or other inner experiences are often handled carelessly or clumsily. I give plenty of examples of this in my booklet on anxiety. If children's brains have good defences, everything that is not handled properly at the time will remain safely wired into the right brain. It is the material that is quarantined in people's right brains that is often behind people's triggers and sensitivities. These are our 'sore toes' that others might step on by accident.

It takes a huge amount of energy to keep stuff quarantined in the right brain, and the more there is the worse it is. This is why people who

---

[28] Parents are allowed to make mistakes as long as they learn from them. If parents acknowledge a mistake and the impact it had on their child, if they apologise to the child, they can restore the trust in the relationship. Parents should learn and grow from their mistakes and not merely repeat the same thing over and over again and apologise over and over again. Parents who get drunk and let their children down regularly or who are repeatedly violent apologise after every incident, damage, rather than build trust, in the relationship. They also make the idea of an apology seem completely meaningless.

have had bad histories and no help at the time, tend to suffer the most. Our development suffers when so much energy is used just to keep what is wired into our right brain from flooding us. But the alternative is to risk damage to the brain.

We have evolved to place physical survival ahead of everything else. This means that long-term developmental tasks are put on the backburner whenever there is a threat to survival. A human with a damaged brain is automatically at risk because they might not be able to perform the necessary to keep themselves alive and well. The brain will therefore wait until the opportunity arises to begin to integrate horizontally without risking physical damage to the brain.

People who come to therapy often have a backlog of quarantined experiences and a feeling that they have missed out on something in their development. A person's history does not always have to include horrific abuse or neglect to cause problems. Anything that is emotionally significant to a child is likely to become quarantined in the right brain if there was no skilled adult response available.

Horizontal integration begins spontaneously when there is enough vertical integration. As you achieve sufficient vertical integration, you might begin to experience strong emotions and memories. These can also come as physical sensations, thoughts, images, dreams or all of the above. This means your brain now feels safe enough to begin to 'release' un-integrated and unprocessed 'raw' experiences from the right brain and connect it to the left. Your natural defences are now relaxing because they are no longer needed.

Horizontal integration cannot and shouldn't be forced or hurried. It happens *by itself* when the brain is good and ready, usually after achieving enough *vertical integration*. Pushing, or forcing ourselves or others to talk about, remember or face things before we feel ready, can lead to re-traumatisation.

Right brain stuff can interfere with most people's functioning in relationships. I often see people who feel impatient with their partners. They realise instinctively that there is something in the partner that is holding them back in the relationship, or causing them to react in ways that are not helpful for the relationship. Sometimes people go to therapy because their partner or someone else has asked them to. But even with

120

the best of intentions, if the brain is not ready it might not work[29]. The idea that people need to be ready to engage with therapy is correct. I hope that when people understand about vertical and horizontal integration, perhaps there will be less fear about going to therapy. But the brain will only engage if it feels it is safe enough to do this.

Our brains and their natural defences can and should be trusted. Our brains know what they are doing. It is OK to say 'no' to a therapist or to someone else who probes into you before you are ready. It is OK to say, 'I do not want to talk about it' if you do not feel ready or feel unsafe with the person in front of you.

You should be in charge of what you are prepared to talk about and face in therapy or elsewhere, and also when and at what pace. You must never allow a therapist to push you or make you feel bad for having defences. Defences are there for an extremely good reason. No one can know the reality of another person's brain. We must always work *with*, *not against* the brain's natural way of operating. The limbic brain is not something to 'beat' or coerce into 'shape', to psychoanalyse, dissect or objectify. In most people it has already suffered enough and it is often full of unprocessed, difficult experiences precisely because of that.

Some people think they have already 'sorted' something and are surprised when it gets triggered again. I've heard many people say, 'But I have already talked about it in therapy. I do not understand why it's still there'. 'Sorted' doesn't necessarily mean integrated. Talking about something with a therapist or thinking about it a lot, understanding how something affected you a certain way does not necessarily or automatically lead to integration. It's nice to understand but the test of integration is in whether or not we have changed permanently.

Neither is catharsis, the experience of strong emotional release, necessarily integration. Sometimes people are capable of releasing something, having a big cry, doing an emotional process in therapy or telling something they've never told before. They do feel some relief but they might be surprised to discover the same familiar triggers are still there.

---

[29] You have no obligation to remain in a bad relationship, especially if you or your children are harmed by your partner. Here I am referring to ordinary situations where people are triggered or trigger one another but where there is no physical or psychological violence and no imbalance of power.

Sometimes we need to process something a few times before it is really 'sorted' or integrated. If there is a lot there, or the original experience is complex, there can be many 'layers' of understanding and 'making sense' of things. I think it just means that the circuitry takes time to get fully integrated. We feel truly 'sorted' and unlikely to be triggered again when the circuitry in the brain is different to how it was before.

Why do we need vertical integration first, before horizontal integration can begin to happen? Vertical integration is the equivalent of a trusted relationship between an adult and a child. Imagine that you are introduced to a child with a bad history and that you are now responsible for this child.

Suppose this child is a survivor from a terrible war and that all they have seen in their short life is a disaster, the kind of things no one, let alone a child, should ever have to witness or experience. What do you do, and how long do you think it would take before the child begins to tell you what happened, what they witnessed and experienced and how they felt?

> Vertical integration provides the safe infrastructure for horizontal integration to begin naturally and organically.

If you work correctly to develop a safe relationship with this child, you would spend as much time as needed validating the child's feelings, while providing for their physical needs and safety. This would gradually make the child feel safe with you, which means the child develops a secure attachment to you.

One day, when the child's brain feels safe enough because you have been consistent and always present and validating, they'll start telling you what happened. This is when you will hear all about the pain and the suffering the child went through. This is when the child might express what it felt like to go through those horrors, what it might have been like to lose his or her mother and father, home, school, friends, their brother or sister, their pet or their favourite toy. The child might cry or rock, appear to re-live some of what they went through even scream. The child would *show* you and *tell* you what it felt like to see the sights they saw, hear the sounds they heard, sense what they sensed.

A safe and trusting relationship between an adult and a child is the equivalent of vertical integration in our adult brain. Once we achieve enough vertical integration for our brain to feel safe and supported internally, the right brain will begin to release what it has quarantined in there, just like the child from the war zone is now ready to speak about, feel and grieve and integrate their experiences.

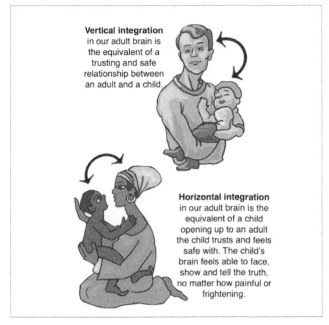

Vertical integration in our adult brain is the equivalent of a trusting and safe relationship between an adult and a child.

Horizontal integration in our adult brain is the equivalent of a child opening up to an adult the child trusts and feels safe with. The child's brain feels able to face, show and tell the truth, no matter how painful or frightening.

Horizontal integration does not make us forget what happened to us. But once something is integrated horizontally, it no longer has the emotional 'charge' it had before. It is much less likely to impact on our wellbeing and development and on how we are in relationships with others.

A therapist cannot be a substitute for your own prefrontal cortex. By interacting with small children, an adult can directly affect their brains and hopefully help them grow up with better integration. Unfortunately, no therapist (or other adult), no matter how capable or well-meaning, can integrate the brain of another adult. Good therapists can only be facilitators. They can provide clients with the environment they need for integration, a trusting and predictable therapeutic relationship, a safe physical environment, the right information and the support they need along the way.

Your own prefrontal cortex has to be *trained* to do what your parents or adult caregivers did not know how to do for you when you were a child. This will enable whatever it is that might be wired into your right brain and is causing you problems, to be properly 'sorted' and integrated once and for all.

Working safely in therapy means focusing first on vertical integration. As vertical integration gets better, the horizontal work will begin spontaneously. That is when people begin to feel and experience more. It does not mean you are going 'backwards' or that you are failing. Rather, now that your limbic brain is feeling more secure and trusting (like our imaginary child from the war zone) it begins to release more.

Even if you feel strong enough, it might still be a good idea to talk to a skilled therapist to support you when the difficult stuff begins to surface. Most well-trained and experienced therapists should be able to sit with you and help you process the difficult material when the time is right. They might have helpful tools or processes and support you to do this more creatively or effectively. Therapists who work on their own integration would understand this and would be safer to work with. If you have a history of trauma or abuse, or you know that you have a troubled limbic brain, it might be a good idea to get the support of a skilled therapist.

If you do not want to work with a therapist it could be helpful to find ways to express yourself such as writing down your feelings or your inner dialogues. Alternatively, you can use any other creative avenue or medium you prefer. The idea is to allow this expression and continue the vertical work while it is happening. This means continuing to breathe and validating everything you feel. Feeling more is not a bad sign. It's a sign that you have been doing a good job with your vertical integration.

The two stages, vertical and horizontal integration, do not always follow one another in a nice and neat order. Sometimes there is a bit of vertical, then horizontal, followed by more vertical and then again more horizontal.

Often horizontal integration will happen in stages after several phases of vertical integration. This can feel 'messy', but if we stay grounded in our understanding of what we are doing, the messy feeling will disappear eventually, and the newly wired brain will offer a much freer, more flexible and more energetic existence.

'Mapping' Our 'Inner World'

The 'Inner Child'

It was a therapist I saw in my late twenties in Sydney who first introduced me to the idea of the inner child. She explained a little bit about what the inner child is, and said that I would have to learn to 'take care of her'. She never went into much detail about how exactly to do this. The idea struck a chord with me at some intuitive level, but I cannot say that I understood what she was talking about.

I also had doubts. To my fairly logical brain, it sounded a bit like 'airy-fairy' New Age stuff. But I was desperate to get better, and a part of me sensed some truth there. I bought some books on the inner child and did my best. I found it difficult and stumbled a lot but to my surprise, it began to make a noticeable difference to me, especially to my levels of anxiety. But I didn't understand how or why this was working.

Most books about the inner child will tell you more or less the same: that you have an inner child inside you, that this inner child contains both your woundedness and all the wonderful qualities in you, such as playfulness, curiosity, creativity, sensuality, capacity for joy and sense of awe, and a desire to learn and experience. They tell you that, in order for you to heal, be well, fully alive and enjoy the benefits that a healthy and free inner child can offer, the inner child has to heal from his or her woundedness. They'll emphasise how liberating it is to acknowledge and embrace your inner child, and how long that child has been waiting to be seen, heard, loved, protected and looked after.

I will not repeat what you can read in many good inner child books. But I would like to show you how the concept of the inner child fits into the model of vertical and horizontal integration. Once you see how it all connects, it will hopefully seem clearer and more accessible to you, and maybe less 'airy fairy' (if you ever thought about it that way).

Many people and even many therapists, consider the inner child to be a kind of a metaphor. If it is a metaphor, then a metaphor for what? What does it actually *mean* that we have something inside our head that is feeling, thinking and behaving like a child? Why can we feel so *child-like* when we are triggered?

From a brain perspective, the inner child is not a metaphor at all. This phrase 'inner child' describes a physical reality in our limbic brain. The inner child is neural circuitry that remained the same throughout the various stages in our development. What we think of as our 'wounded' inner child is brain circuitry that hasn't integrated properly. It may contain unprocessed hurt feelings from our past that have been safely quarantined in our right brain. In reality we all have more than one inner child. There is likely to be a whole host of 'inner characters' inside of us. They are all unintegrated neural circuits from different significant moments in our development.

How many inner 'characters' we each have, and what they are, depends on our individual experience of growing up and also on other factors such as our society and culture. The 'inner world', 'inner characters', our 'inner landscape' is a product of significant times or events that had an important emotional impact on us. There will be as many inner 'characters' as the number of emotionally significant experiences in people's history that were not handled skilfully by adults and were not helped to integrate at the time. The more painful and traumatic the experience was, the more 'quarantined' or isolated the relevant circuitry will be. The isolation of each cluster of neurons mirrors the isolation we in fact faced at that moment in our history.

Even if we cannot remember a lot from our past, and even if we cannot remember every significant moment, our brain circuitry does not lie. If it's there, it has a good reason to be there. These neural circuits developed in direct response to our environment and what happened to us. Our brain reflects our environment. Whatever was on the outside will end up on the inside...

As I explained earlier, we need particular emotional engagement and relationships from the significant adults around us in order for integrative fibres to form between our brains, both vertically and horizontally. When these relationships are not available, the emotional impact of these events or experiences doesn't integrate. It remains in the relevant circuitry, and stays as it is despite the passage of time, and despite the fact that our bodies and other parts of our brain continue to grow into adulthood.

This is why people do not feel any better in the long term just from time passing, from moving away or growing up. Unless old circuitry has integrated, there is no reason for us to feel any different than we have felt in the past. We take our brain with us everywhere we go and our past will always be with us and will affect us until we integrate it.

These bits of neural circuitry from different times in our earlier life, (our 'inner young selves') stay there 'waiting'. They can act like regenerating 'landmines'. When they're triggered, they fire along the same patterns they did when we *were* those ages and lived through those times and experiences. As a result, we end up feeling exactly as we did at the age when that neural network was created at the time of the original event or events.

Our Inner Dynamic

The inner relationships and dialogues that are in our heads shape our inner experience and our outer behaviour. I sometimes use experiential methods in my work, such as psychodrama, to help my clients 'see' their inner dynamic more clearly. Experiential therapy or 'action methods' enable clients to take what is inside their heads and act it out safely. Clients who experience this for the first time are often surprised by the experience. They also recognise it as exactly what happens inside their heads. Siegel says that

> Optimal self-organization arose when the system was having two interactive processes occur. One was differentiating elements of the system, allowing them to become unique and have their own integrity; the other was linking these differentiated elements of the system. The common term we could use for this linkage of differentiated parts was integration.
> – Daniel Siegel. Mind: A Journey to the Heart of Being Human. (p.78)

Working with our 'inner characters' demonstrates this principle of differentiation and integration beautifully. With or without a therapist, people can learn to recognise the 'characters' (or as some call it, inner 'parts') that are wired into their limbic brain. They can also recognise and access their 'adult' in the prefrontal cortex. In therapy we train the prefrontal cortex to become the parent we might not have had[30].

Once all our inner parts are seen clearly, once they are acknowledged as separate, differentiated parts and are given a clear voice, they can be integrated. Integration means creating the correct relationship between those parts and the 'parent character' in the prefrontal cortex. This means that the prefrontal cortex can begin to take its rightful role in the client's brain.

In most of the clients I have seen, and certainly in myself, I have found that there are two dominant inner parts that tend to present themselves in therapy. These are a very young version of the person, a small child, and a teenager-like version.

The younger child 'character' tends to experience and express feelings like sadness, helplessness, shame and fear. The teenager or adolescent version of the person tends to be the 'pseudo-adult'. It's the part of us that tries to act like an adult based on the role models we had available to us in our adolescence. If the adults around us were ultra-logical, distant, impatient, critical or harsh, this is what the inner adolescent is likely to be like as well. If the adults were chaotic and irresponsible, the inner teenager would behave the same way. As teenagers we imitate whatever adult role models are available to us because we are trying to learn how to be adults. We do not just imitate what is done to us. We also imitate what we see the adults do to themselves and to each other.

Teenagers can be rebellious if they feel that people around them place obstacles in their path to developing their identity and becoming independent. Teenagers can be, and often are, competent and adult-like. They want and need to be respected for their developing skills and abilities. If real adults are not available in a family, it's often a teenager who would step up to look after younger siblings and take care of things that should otherwise be the responsibility of parents. However, teenagers are still young themselves and are still developing. They need to be supported and guided. They do not need close care, like small children, but they do still need to know someone cares and has their back.

---

[30] When parents interact correctly with their children they train the child's prefrontal cortex to be the inner parent. As the child grows up they internalise that safe and connected parent. But if this did not happen in childhood, we have to do this as adults.

Teenagers lack life experience and the emotional resilience to cope with adult responsibilities. They are still largely limbic, so still need safety, approval, a sense of belonging and a lot of respectful guidance. They might appear selfish and can lack empathy, or rather their empathy will be unreliable. They might not know how to balance caring for others with caring for themselves. If circumstances require that they care for others, they are likely to feel overwhelmed and resentful while trying to rise to the challenge and appear competent.

Although teenagers can take a lot of responsibility, they would feel more motivated, safe and worry-free if they could rely on competent mature adults to be in charge. They do not need to be micromanaged, but they need to know that it's not all up to them, and that if they make mistakes it won't be the end of the world. If this is not available, they are likely to feel overwhelmed, let down, frightened, angry, and if they feel powerless to make a difference to their circumstances, they can get depressed.[31]

If feelings were not handled correctly when we were growing up; if sadness, anger, pain, jealousy, hatred, disappointment or fear, for example, were criticised, dismissed or labelled 'weak' or 'wrong', this is what adolescents would learn to say to themselves and to others. To appear competent, adolescents would deny or push away the suffering of their inner 'younger self'. They simply learn from what is around them. I believe adolescence is often one of the loneliest and scariest periods in a lot of people's lives.

In the absence of mature, integrated and skilled adults around us in childhood, we grow into adults whose limbic brain is forced to 'parent' itself. This just mirrors the reality in which we grew up. Our prefrontal cortex never learned to 'parent' our limbic brain, so our limbic brain continues to do its best to parent itself, largely disconnected from the part of us that is supposed to be the inner parent. This is another way of looking at 'coping'.

In our adult brain, our *inner teenager* will try to 'parent' our younger inner child just like we did when we were that age. The harsher or more

---

[31] I have always believed that half the problems people experience with teenagers have to do with the fact that the teenager can sense that the adults in their lives are not really adult. Why would a sixteen-year-old obey or respect someone they sense is the same age as they are, sometimes even less? It is terrifying to wake up into self-awareness at age fifteen only to realise there is no one there to give you real guidance. I am not surprised so many teenagers go through such a hard time — that is in addition to the expected hormonal and life changes they go through.

emotionally clumsy the environment was, or if we were left to deal with our emotions mostly on our own, the worse our inner teenager would treat itself and the inner child. As a result, there will be tension or even 'warfare' inside. This is the state most people are in when they first come to therapy.

No inner part of us is bad. There is no 'inner critic' or 'saboteur'. I find this terminology, which is used in many self-help books, deeply unfair and unhelpful. None of our inner parts are the 'enemy' to control or defeat or 'bend into shape'. In the absence of a proper inner adult 'parent', inner children and teenagers are just doing their best to survive, fending for themselves and dealing with their fears as best they can and with the skills they have managed to learned. They are like children and young people left on their own, still waiting for someone to take charge, take care of them and take care of things.

Adults who parent their children from their inner adolescent do not provide role modelling for an integrated brain. Their children would then grow into adults whose limbic brain is in conflict with itself. I find that the more abusive people's history was, the more toxic and troubled the *inner* conflict tends to be.

If people's childhood environment was relatively safe and peaceful, the inner conflict would tend to be less dramatic or torturous. But without good integration between the limbic brain and the prefrontal cortex, there will always be some degree of inner tension, turmoil or conflict. People can, and do cope with a great deal while living with this inner conflict, but at a price. When life hits particularly hard, or demands increase, people's limbic coping mechanisms can reach their limits. It is usually in times like this that people come to therapy. They can feel like a time of crisis but it's a useful signal from the brain that integrative work is needed.

Typical Inner 'Landscape' at the Start of Therapy

What isn't said out loud
I'm scared I can't do it
I'm a fraud. I'm scared I'll be found out
I can't show my real feelings
I don't want people to think I'm weak
I don't want people to think I'm stupid
I need someone to tell me what to do
I'm exhausted, I can't cope any more
I need a break.

Go Away!
I can't stand you
You're annoying
I'm stuck because of you
SHUT UP!
SHUT UP!
I don't have time for this
You're pathetic!
You're weak
You're making me fail
Just get on with it
You're making me feel bad
You're disgusting

Inner Child
I'm scared
I'm lonely
I need someone to look afer me
I need someone to hug me
I need someone to tell me it's
going to be OK
I'm always causing trouble
I want to play
I want to have fun
I have to do what he/she says
I don't want to do it
I hate myself
I'm ugly
I'm fat
I'm stupid
I'm a loser
I'm ashamed

Inner Teenager
I'm pissed off
I don't give a shit
I can cope
Leave me alone
I don't need therapy
I don't need anyone to tell me what to do
It's all stupid anyway
I don't trust anyone
I don't need anyone

- The worse the upbringing was, the worse this inner dynamic tends to be.
- People who have had OK childhoods tend to be far less conflicted within themselves.

I am a private practitioner, so the clients I see are people who are well-functioning. Their external lives are more or less in order and they are able to pay for private therapy. I think that most functional people who suffer from stress and anxiety operate out of their inner teenager. It's the most adult-like part that has developed in most of us.

I have always thought that people whose lives are chaotic; people who are unable to manage even the basics of life, probably operate out of a much younger inner child. If you think about putting a small child in charge of things, you are likely to end up with some degree of chaos. Children always try to do their best but they are not equipped for high levels of responsibility. There is likely to be fear and panic and plenty of unsound, erratic decisions.

In the early days of my practice, when I tried to teach clients about inner child work, a small number were able to do this without any problem. They would quickly begin to feel compassion for their inner child. They would understand what it felt and what it needed and were able to provide this.

However, the majority of my clients had problems with this. They would return session after session reporting feeling impatient and annoyed with 'the little brat' inside their head. They would say things like 'I hate the snivelling little thing. She is so weak and pathetic. Why cannot she grow up?' Or simply, 'I just couldn't do it and got fed up'. Many of these people seemed irritated and even ashamed of their inner child. It became clear to me that something wasn't right. I then started to wonder *who* it was exactly in them that was trying to 'parent' their inner child. The words that people used, the sentiments they expressed, their facial expressions and body language reminded me of how teenagers can be. I then started to wonder if it was the teenager part of my clients that was trying to 'parent' the child. It was then that I realised something was missing.

The clients who were instinctively able to embrace their younger child and care for him or her, sounded and looked different. I noticed that the small number of people who were able to do this relatively easily did not have a history of childhood abuse. They didn't have perfect childhoods, but they did not suffer from any form of trauma. The majority who found it hard to do, tended to have difficult childhoods. Many of them suffered abuse and had varying degrees of trauma. But they were 'copers' and survivors. Their lives were difficult but they were able to hold jobs and more or less function, albeit at a cost.

I began to realise that in the clients who found this work difficult it was the limbic brain that was trying to parent itself. In terms of the inner relationship nothing had really changed. The teenager was trying to be nicer, thinking it had to be the 'adult' in the brain because the therapist said so. But it couldn't do it so nothing changed. If the architecture of the brain, the inner 'landscape' does not change, there is no reason why people should feel any different to how they have always felt.

The inner child (or rather children) doesn't need to 'grow up' and neither does the inner teenager. The limbic brain will always be the limbic brain. But in order to function well it needs to integrate with the 'adult' in the prefrontal cortex, with the executive brain, which is made for this job.

The inner child work I was trying to facilitate with my clients was not so productive until I realised that it was the prefrontal cortex that has to learn to take care of the child or children within. If we do not train the prefrontal cortex to do this, we won't achieve much. You can give other people's limbic brains some relief by providing validation and acceptance from the outside. But without change to brain architecture, without integration inside a client's brains, any relief in the limbic brain will be short-lived and the original problems will resurface. Without proper integration, the executive brain will not be in charge reliably and the younger selves in the limbic brain will continue to have to 'parent' themselves.

The rebellious generation of the 1960s did not lead to a real revolution in the long term. I have read somewhere that it is that generation that later led to even more conservatism in the world and brought corporate power and greed to their current levels. The 'flower children' or 'hippies' were different from the mainstream in their time and from their parents' generation because they were able to listen to their inner younger child and its longing for love, warmth and expression in life. They used their inner teenager's sense of justice and rebellious spirit to motivate them into action against the evils of the establishment in their time. But they did not go on to integrate. As a result, their actions were not sustainable. In the longer term, it was the more 'sensible' and 'realistic' inner teenager that took over in their lives and drove them to a more ruthless set of values rather than to the fulfilment of what their inner child wanted.

A suggestion to help develop your awareness of your inner 'characters':

Each time use the word 'I', pause for a moment, breathe and ask yourself which 'I' in you is speaking.

A Safe 'Meeting Place' or a Safe Space

There is an exercise that has long been suggested in self-help books or meditations on the inner-child that I have always found helpful. I think it has a great deal of value provided it is not too prescriptive. People should allow themselves to develop their own images rather than be told what to imagine. So, feel free to let your mind guide you through this.

As you get to know your inner 'characters' and begin to develop a relationship with them, it might help to have regular 'meetings' at a 'safe place'. It can help to imagine or think about a safe place you like or are drawn to. It can be a real or imaginary place, an image you saw somewhere or a combination.

I have an image that I created from a scene in a Star Trek episode. It's on a beach at night. There is a lovely fire pit in the middle and the dark starry sky stretches above. I and my inner world sit in a circle around the fire pit and everyone is welcome to say or feel whatever they need to. I used to use this image sometimes just before situations that I felt could trigger me or that characters within me were dreading. This exercise allowed me to have a safe meeting and a 'debrief' before the real task. It is no different from what a good manager or team leader would do when they know their team is about to face something difficult or challenging.

Imagining that beach scene where everyone is equal and everyone is safe to express themselves, I was able to listen to all the parts of myself, validate 'their' feeling and concerns and reassure them that I, the executive, am in charge and will handle everything that we have to face. This exercise contributes to ongoing long-term integration because of the focused dialogue between the brains. In the shorter term, it provides the focus we need to face a potentially difficult task.

A variation on this exercise can be useful when you deal with a particularly frightened younger version of yourself who might have experienced an unsafe environment in your past. It helps to ask this version of you where he or she would like to go and then 'take them' there. This is the equivalent of taking a suffering child from a place that is harmful to them and bringing them to a place where they are safe from harm and can relax and get on with being a child. Children should never have to go back to a frightening and unsafe environment and neither should those parts of our limbic brain that are wired from our past. As we repeat this exercise, we wire a new inner space and make it safer inside our own brain.

As I mentioned above you can do this in writing, as a dialogue between your different 'parts'. If you are artistic you can draw or sculpt this as well. A skilled Psychodrama or Gestalt psychotherapist can help you facilitate this in a therapy session in a way that will enable you to act out the inner conversation and 'create' the safe space using art or props in the therapy room.

Over time you won't need to do this in such an elaborate way, because the connections between your brains will become permanent. Your two brains will work well together all the time, just like a team of people functions well in the knowledge that there is a manager who listens and who is in charge of everything.

Ingenuity Without Ethics – The Danger of Unintegrated Brains

> For the first time ever, one species—with the questionable self-label the "wise humans"—has the awesome power to threaten the health, perhaps even the survival of all species. Using our superb intellectual endowment, this species has created and misused technology, squandered limited natural resources, and multiplied in unrestrained ways so that the earth's biosphere is being depleted more rapidly than it can repair itself by natural processes. ... Doing everything we can to maximize our individual and family health obviously is very important. But to focus only on maintaining personal health while ignoring the social causes of much illness in todays' world, is increasingly inadequate.
>
> – Howard Clinebell, Ecotherapy: Healing Ourselves, Healing the Earth. 1996.

This chapter is my commentary on what happens to us as groups and societies when we are not well integrated. It is important to me not to give the impression that all I'm interested in is offering yet another individualistic, self-centred self-help book. We cannot be OK as individuals if what is around us is not OK and vice versa. We and the world around us are part of an interconnected complex system.

What we call 'therapy' and 'mental health' are never just about individuals. When our two brains are not well connected, it does not just affect how we are and what we do as individuals, but also how we are as families, groups and societies. One of the most important lessons we already know and which has been confirmed by neuroscience, is that we do not develop in isolation. We are born as a result of relationships and depend on relationships for our survival. Regardless of our genetic potential, it is the quality of the relationships we are offered when we are brought up and throughout our lives that determines how we turn out. *Everything* about us, how our brains are wired and our minds, is a product of relationships.

When we are not well integrated, everything in our brain will be working in the service of survival. It will not be for our executive brain's need to live with purpose, meaning, ethics, inclusivity and universal values. If our executive and limbic functions are not well connected, all the ingenuity we can get from the rest of our modern brain will end up working in the service of a competitive, fear-based primate who cares a great deal about surviving another day but not much else.

Lack of sufficient integration is what enables brilliant scientists, scholars, inventors, philosophers, lawyers, politicians, doctors, engineers, teachers and many other highly educated people to use their knowledge and expertise for wrong, or even outright evil purposes.

It was scientists and doctors who worked to find the most efficient mass killing methods for the Nazi regime. They first experimented on intellectually disabled people whom they considered expendable and not worth living, and then used the technology on Jews, Gypsies, homosexuals, Catholics, people of colour, Jehovah's Witnesses and anyone else the regime they worked for wanted to exterminate. It was doctors who certified the mass deaths in the death camps.

Psychologists and psychiatrists in many countries carry out torture for the governments they work for. Incredibly smart scientists spend all of their time developing more sophisticated ways for us to kill one another and destroy our planet. Countless scientists and science students all over the world participate daily in the torture and murder of innocent sentient (feeling) animals, telling themselves that what they are doing is OK because it is for the benefit of our species' medicine or survival. These are the people who work within the law. (There are of course many smart criminals who use their knowledge and expertise to steal and scam people exploiting our increasingly digital world). Too many professionals sell their time and ingenuity in the service of things that harm others. They are directly responsible for our many problems and they are supported and even valued by our economic system.

A number of scientists and inventors throughout history have regretted what they created with their genius. The list includes Robert Oppenheimer, leader of the US Manhattan Project that developed the atomic bomb. In 1945, when he realised the monstrosity he helped create, Oppenheimer met with President Harry S. Truman and tried to convince him to ban the use of atomic weapons. But there was no going back, the genie was out of the bottle. The evil he had helped create was in place and it was used to destroy Hiroshima and Nagasaki and cripple and traumatise generations of Japanese people. Experimentation with the impact of nuclear radiation on people carried out by doctors and scientists continued long after the end of the Second World War.[32]

Albert Einstein, whose ground-breaking work in theoretical physics made the atomic bomb possible, considered it his greatest mistake in hindsight, but not before he himself suggested the project to the US government. The Swedish scientist and businessman Alfred Nobel, known for creating the famous Nobel Peace Prize, invented dynamite and regretted it. Mikhail Kalashnikov invented the automatic assault rifle, then expressed deep regret a year before his death in 2013.

Too little, too late? If all these extraordinarily talented people were able to use their PFC *at the same time* as they felt excited and curious about some new idea or invention and about being given plenty of funding to carry out their work, they could have anticipated the outcome of their clever inventions. If they had been able to use their executive to consider the impact of what they were doing; if they had thought about the kind of people to whom they were giving these inventions *before* they went ahead with their projects, they would have refused. If they had been able to slow down, breathe and think more clearly, they might have been able to engage their ethics before, not after, they did what they did.

These are examples of people who were able to recognise their mistakes in hindsight. But plenty of smart people are doing bad things right now and are not giving it a second thought. It is not OK for people to work without ethics and without considering how their creations or ideas might be used. It is not OK for people to not care about the impact of their work.

The more educated and knowledgeable people are, the more dangerous they and their work can be, if the ethics-related part of their brain is not engaged[33]. Smart and educated people have a great deal of

---

[32] See John Pilger's documentary *The Coming War on China* – available for free on his website – for what the US did in the Bikini Atoll. Well-educated and bright doctors, scientists, engineers and technicians were in charge of those experiments. Without these highly qualified people these would not have been possible. This demonstrates how ingenuity without the ethics and empathy of the PFC and in the services of our limbic chimpanzee makes us effectively evil.

[33] There is such a thing as ethicists who are trying to alert scientists and legislators to the potential consequences of different types of research. In each country there are areas of research that are banned. But it is always an ongoing battle. It would not be a battle if the scientists themselves were able to think in advance about the consequences of what they are doing and make

influence because the knowledge and technology they produce have a global impact. No evil or misguided leader can do their work or fulfil their fantasies on their own. They always have help and collaboration from smart and educated people. It is those people who can transform crazy, dangerous ideas into reality and who fulfil the depraved or irresponsible fantasies of people with political power.

Some smart people who do bad things are psychopaths. They intend to harm others and they enjoy it. But most people are not psychopathic, certainly not those from the above list who expressed regrets about their projects. They were just ordinary humans who suffered from the same problems we all have. They were not sufficiently integrated.

What we instinctively call psychological maturity is directly related to integration. The more integrated we are, the more mature we will be. A mistake many people make is to assume that a person who is a scientist, a doctor or a university professor is also mature psychologically. Being smart or well-educated does not automatically mean being well-integrated.

You can tell when smart or educated people are not well integrated when they hide behind authority and justify themselves with 'I feel fine about what I am doing because I am helping my country', 'I am only following orders' or 'I'm only doing my job'. You can also tell by looking at who they work for. People who are better integrated would not work for the wrong people. They are also prepared to speak out when they feel they are asked to do something in the service of an unethical or harmful organisation or project. Speaking out is hard on the limbic brain. Our limbic brain seeks the group's approval and does not want to 'upset the applecart', it would worry about its own income, status and survival. But when people are better integrated, they are able to feel uncomfortable feelings and do the right thing anyway.

Some of the most prestigious projects in the world today are used for harmful purposes, such as military technology or the oppression of people. Only a well-integrated, ethical individual can resist the temptation of a big salary and the status that working for a big multinational company or a government can offer. That is because properly integrated brains are run and managed by the executive brain,

---

ethical choices themselves. There are those who do but for every scientist that opts out, there are a hundred others who would lend their knowledge and expertise to technologies that ultimately harm us.

140

which is naturally inclusive and ethical. Our in-built prefrontal ethics tells us that everyone and everything matters, not just our own bank balance, our group, family, tribe, society or country, and that we should harm no one, no matter what.

Young humans are looking to adults for guidance on how to live in the world. But all they see when they look at the world is a big frightening mess. Most of them adapt because they have no choice if they want to carve a little bit of life for themselves. They have every right to expect that those who are running things, the people we elect to manage and run our countries and societies, know what they are doing. But observant and intelligent young people can easily see that grownups do not know better than they do. When I was young I was often told I was 'too idealistic' and that by the time I turned forty I would 'grow out of it'. As you can see, I have not. If anything, I am much more idealistic now than I have ever been. Idealism is a big part of what motivates my work as a therapist.

Once you understand that our limbic and executive functions are naturally poorly integrated; once you understand that most parents do not know how to help their children's brains integrate, I think the answer is clear. The human world is run mostly on limbic impulses. Because most of us are poorly integrated and are dominated by our limbic functions, we are only able to create societies in our own image, that of an ingenious but tribal, territorial, short-sighted, frightened and often ruthless primate.

We just have to look around us, turn on the TV or read the newspapers. Fear and constant drama sell news, and competition and scarcity are the norm. We know from our recorded history that things have always been this way. Might has always been 'right' no matter what gloss we choose to put on it. The only difference is that our immense technological advances are enabling us to do more harm and on a larger scale than ever before. In other words, as a species we have grown worse, not better.

We aren't bad *per se* and this is not even about 'good' or 'bad'. But when we run life from our mammal brain, we allow fear and our unconscious drive for the survival of our species to run our existence. Or rather, we seem to be focused on little more than physical existence.

Paradoxically, short-term limbic thinking and individual selfishness are now bringing us closer to our extinction than ever before[34].

Remember that the limbic brain's imagination is limited by its experience. Anything beyond our experience can seem impossible, a 'pipe dream'. The 'real world', as so many people call it, is not run by our executive drive to grow, to be fulfilled and live with purpose and meaning, by the desire to be kind to others and do the right thing by everyone. When we are limbic we cannot see beyond our own noses and beyond our own fears. We are easily led by the politics of what we believe is 'possible' and most people do not know how to see beyond it.

We like to think we are rational and that we make rational choices. We glorify a lot of what we do with complex theories and justifications. But it seems to me that our species has created for itself a nightmarish world that mirrors our past hardships, the old jungle where our limbic brain has evolved; a world of dangers, unpredictability, scarcity, death and constant threat and fear. Because our limbic brain cannot imagine anything that we have not already experienced either individually, or as a species, we end up (mostly) recreating and repeating what we know. I say 'mostly' because it's not all bad and there is plenty of good out there too. But the overall picture is truly appalling and does not do justice to what we are capable of creating.

If we do not integrate as individuals and as societies, we condemn ourselves to replay our past experiences over and over again. When we are not well integrated what we learn from our experience is how to survive, not how to grow and develop. To do better we have to imagine better, and the only part of our brain that can imagine the unimaginable and make it possible is our PFC. But in order to run our lives from this amazing bit of brain we have, it must be integrated better with our

---

[34] I have recently watched David Attenborough's excellent 2020 documentary *A Life On Our Planet*. The title intends to indicate that this is Attenborough's personal testimony following a lifetime and a career exposing us to our relationship with our natural environment. In his lifetime Attenborough has witnessed the unprecedented destruction of our natural environment entirely by our own hands. But he is hopeful that we can still do something about it and that we can turn things around if we act right now. He makes excellent suggestions based on programmes that already exist in some areas around the world and that demonstrate what is possible if the will to act is there. We will not make any positive difference to anything as long as we continue to operate from our limbic brain, or rather continue to use our ingenuity in the service of our survivalist brain instead of the compassionate and inclusive executive. Paradoxically, using our ingenuity in the service of a brain that just wants our species to survive, is precisely the thing that is likely to lead to our extinction. The documentary is available on Netflix and I cannot recommend it enough.

limbic functions. When we are each integrated better we can help young people integrate better and so lead to a new generation of more integrated human beings. When we are better integrated we would no longer put up with societies that focus only on survival and create conditions that force us into survival. We would be able to create societies that are organised around the fulfilment of everyone's potential.

A Few Last Words

It is hard to write a short book. There are difficult choices to make about what to include and what to leave out. My guide for this book has been the process I use with my clients, and I hope I have made reasonable choices.

If you are a parent, grandparent, teacher, or someone who is involved with children's development in any capacity, integrating your own brain should be a priority. As you integrate your brain, you will have a profound growth-promoting impact on young people. You will also find that the work of raising and guiding children and young people (and all other tasks in your life for that matter) will flow with more ease. It will also be much more fulfilling and inspiring for everyone.

We can only model what we really are and where we are in our development. Children and young people yearn to develop into everything they are capable of becoming, and need well-integrated adults to help them. Young people do not know how to ask for what they need. When we are young, we instinctively expect those around us to know how to guide us, not just to survive but to become fully human.

When adults operate mostly from their limbic brains, they are reactive and not present enough psychologically. Young people have no choice but to adapt to their environment, but they feel lonely, angry, and scared. Young humans do not know how to say to the adults in their life, 'Please validate my feelings because I need to know that you know what my limbic brain is worried about.' 'Please tell me you have my back and you will keep me safe.' 'Please tell me everything will turn out alright'... But these are precisely the things that every child or young person needs to hear all the time. Most of my clients used to be young people who did not get what they needed to develop more fully. If everyone helped young humans to develop properly, psychotherapy would become obsolete. We can then get on living in a peaceful world where everyone grows and everyone's life is fulfilling and inspiring.

Parenting children with a well-integrated brain is much easier than trying to parent them from our reactive limbic brain. Our limbic brain can teach children how to survive. But our executive brain is what guides them, and models to them how to be fully human.

I hope I have managed to communicate a coherent framework that can help you make sense of your feelings and behaviour, and understand the tools for integration. I wanted to show that therapy does not need to be 'airy fairy', that real change in our psychology happens inside our brain, and that it depends on connecting key brain systems better.

As you finish reading this book, I hope you will feel better informed, and more empowered to ask for what you need. Whether you are allocated a therapist by a service, or choose a therapist for yourself, you can now ask informed questions about how they work, and how it would benefit you.

Last but not least, our bodies, brains, minds are a complex system. Complex systems are bigger than the sum of their parts, and everything in them interacts with everything else. Your body is not a mindless object, it may even be conscious. (Evidence from biology begins to point to the fact that cells in our body may well be conscious[35]).

When people are not well integrated, when their suffering limbic brain is at the helm, they might not look after themselves particularly well. When the mind feels like it is in a state of constant warfare, the body is often treated like an enemy.

I have consistently found that as we integrate better, we naturally treat our bodies better. We instinctively begin to do things that we might have known we should do but could not. When we are better integrated, we do the right things, because we want to. We listen better to the messages from our body, and we naturally want to look after this aspect of our being.

Because we are a system, *everything* about us is inter-connected, and in relationship with everything else. Anywhere or any time you intervene in any system – for better or worse – it would have an impact on the whole system, for better or worse. That is why you can make

---

[35] See for example:

1) 'The social nature of mitochondria: Implications for human health' by Martin Picard_and Carmen Sandi in the journal *Neuroscience & Biobehavioral Reviews*. Volume 120, January 2021, Pages 595-610.

2) 'Cells in confinement and people in crowds have similar behaviors, shows study' by Maureen Searcy, 28 July 2023 in phys.org (the link to the original journal article is at the bottom of the phys.org repor)t.

conscious changes to how you treat your body at any time, for example, and you will see a difference.

Everything about us matters, and our approach should not be based on a choice between the body *or* the mind. It is both, and much more. Please do not give yourself a hard time if you cannot change habits in the short term. Keep integrating your brain, and you will notice that changes begin to happen naturally.

Science is only scratching the surface of understanding human beings as systems. The current approach to both physical and mental health is still compartmentalised, or reductionistic, not systemic. Only a systemic science can address us as systems. But we are not there yet.

Science treats physical and psychological problems in isolation. Perhaps because the human world is predominantly driven by our limbic instincts, we a war-like mentality about our physical and mental health. Treatments tend to be based on 'fighting' something to 'defeat' or 'eliminate' it, often with little understanding of, or interest in the whole system. This approach can make existing problems worse. If it solves a problem in one area, it can lead to a new problem or problems in other areas.

The mind-body divide is imaginary. The placebo effect is accounted for in every study in medicine, and also in psychology. In other words, *mainstream science* knows and recognises that the mind can heal and change the body. No one in the mainstream is studying placebo, and inexplicably, the mind is largely ignored in medicine.

Always use knowledge in combination with your own observations, and understanding of yourself. Do not listen to or follow blindly anyone's advice, including mine. Whenever you learn something new, be sure to refer to your own innate wisdom to tell you what makes sense to you and what doesn't. Listen to the feedback your mind and body offer you continuously, and adjust what you do and how you treat yourself accordingly. Integration means listening to everything that our minds and bodies tell us, and ensuring that the system that is us works in flow and harmony.

I wish you well with your work to integrate and grow.

About the author

Avigail Abarbanel has been a psychotherapist in private practice since 1999. She started practising in Australia, and in 2010 moved to the Scottish Highlands, where she re-established her practice, 'Fully Human Psychotherapy'.

Avigail is Snr Accredited with the BACP. She works with adult individuals, relationships and groups. She is also a supervisor, trainer, consultant, and writer. Avigail is passionate about sharing everything she knows, and about removing the mystery and mystique out of mental health and therapy. She has healthy curiosity and many interests, but never enough time to pursue them all…

Please visit **http://fullyhuman.co.uk** for more information.

Registered Member **16797**
MBACP (Snr Accred)

Printed in Great Britain
by Amazon

31075459R00088